IFRS Simplified:

A fast and easy to understand overview of the new
International Financial Reporting Standards

IFRS
Simplified

A fast and easy to understand overview of the new
International Financial Reporting Standards

Michel Morley, CPA

Nixon-Carre Ltd., Toronto, ON

Library and Archives Canada Cataloguing in Publication

Morley, Michel, 1952-
   IFRS Simplified: a fast and easy to understand overview of the new international financial reporting standards / Michel Morley.

Includes index.
ISBN 978-0-9783939-1-5

   1. Accounting--Standards. I. Title.
HF5626.M67 2009   657.02'18   C2008-906344-9

Published by:
Nixon-Carre Ltd.
P.O. Box 92533
Carlton RPO
Toronto, Ontario, M5A 4N9
www.nixon-carre.com

Distributed by Ingram

Contents

Chapter 8 - IAS and IFRS Summaries cont.

Introduction

Like it or not, the accounting rules in North America are about to change!

Researching the new International Financial Reporting Standards for my clients was a painful task. Continually searching through long, difficult to read technical manuals it became obvious to me that there was a need for an easy-to-understand, concise introduction to IFRS.

I have tried to translate the technical accounting language into plain English so that everyone can understand the new accounting rules that will soon apply to "publicly accountable enterprises" in North America.

"IFRS Simplified" provides a jump start for accountants and finance executives who want to quickly and easily get up to date on IFRS.

However, since International Financial Reporting Standards are rules that are constantly being reviewed and updated to meet the changing needs of investors, if you have a specific question as to whether the Standard that you are using is current check with your auditor.

GAAP vs. IFRS 1

GAAP has worked great up to now, why change things?

Although North American publicly traded companies are presently preparing their financial statements according to Generally Accepted Accounting Principles (GAAP), this is quickly changing. Canada is moving to IFRS based statements effective January 1, 2011, and the chairman of the SEC announced a roadmap to achieve IFRS compliance in the USA by 2014.

Even companies that are not legally required to comply with IFRS will feel strong pressure to adapt to the new worldwide standards. This is especially true of private companies wanting to merge with large public firms and companies that are suppliers to international IFRS compliant firms.

GAAP has been with us for many years and is not being abandoned. GAAP will continue to be used for some time after the official switch to IFRS.

So what's the difference between GAAP and IFRS?

GAAP is rules based while IFRS is principles based. What this means is that IFRS provides more flexible guidelines for choosing what to include in (and what to leave out of) the financial statements while GAAP imposes more rigid rules. IFRS requires more judgment decisions on the part of the accountants, but provides more flexibility to explain unique situations.

Another important difference between GAAP and IFRS is that GAAP measures assets at historical cost (the original purchase price of the asset), while IFRS can measure assets in terms of their potential future benefits for the company. For example, a painting originally purchased for $1000 to decorate the lobby of a building, but which is now appraised at more than $100,000 would, under GAAP, continue to be recorded at its original $1000 cost, while, under IFRS, the value of the asset would be increased to reflect its fair market value, thus making the increase in the value of the company visible to the investor.

Investors have been demanding this changeover in order to be able to more easily compare international investing opportunities.

Who needs to comply?

"Publicly Accountable Enterprises" in the 25 countries of the European Union as well as Australia, New Zealand, South Africa, Russia, China, and many other countries are already required to produce IFRS financial statements. "Publicly Accountable Enterprises" in the USA and Canada will require IFRS compliance shortly.

"Publicly Accountable Enterprises" are companies that hold assets in a fiduciary capacity. In other words, they are companies that hold public money "in trust", such as banks, insurance companies, and companies whose shares are traded on a public stock exchange, such as the London Stock Exchange, the New York Stock Exchange, and the NASDAQ.

The Benefits of IFRS

Standardization

The push to change from GAAP to IFRS has primarily come from large international companies wanting to have a universal method of producing financial statements. IFRS financial statements are faster and less expensive for these companies to produce because the accounting staff of a multi-national company will not have to be familiar with all the variations of GAAP in the different countries in which the company operates. Another advantage is that IFRS makes it easier for companies to develop a common system for internal management accounting reports.

Investor confidence

IFRS promotes investor confidence by requiring better explanatory notes to the financial statements. Since IFRS requires more judgment decisions in choosing how to record the value of liabilities, assets, and equity, explanations describing how those judgments were made are also required.

In other words, the notes need to explain why the choices were made.

Substance over form

The principle of "substance over form" means that clarity is the primary consideration. Investors must feel confident that the financial statements are providing them with a true and fair presentation of the company's financial condition.

Facilitating the free flow of capital

IFRS makes financial statements easier to compare. Since investors tend to put their money into companies and investments that they understand, having clear IFRS financial statements available makes decision making easier.

IFRS makes it easier for companies to be listed on foreign stock exchanges. The ability to get listed on foreign stock exchanges gives companies access to additional investors. Most foreign stock exchanges either require or accept IFRS financial statements.

IFRS vs. SOX

The implementation of IFRS does not affect Sarbanes-Oxley (SOX).

Sarbanes-Oxley is the law that makes executives of publicly traded US companies personally and criminally responsible for their company's financial statements and disclosures. In other words, SOX is about making executives accountable for the reliability of the financial statements while IFRS is about the rules for preparing the financial statements.

Until recently, SOX demanded that audited financial statements prepared using US GAAP must be filed with the SEC. However, the SEC recently announced that it is now accepting IFRS based audited statements in addition to US GAAP statements.

Deadlines

The deadline for comparative IFRS financial statements for "Publicly Accountable Enterprises" in the USA is January 1, 2014 and January 1, 2011 in Canada. To meet these requirements the company will have to have IFRS systems in place one year in advance in order to produce the required two years of comparative figures in the financial statements.

IFRS 1 requires that the first year adopters of IFRS must start with a comparative balance sheet that converts it from GAAP to IFRS. It also requires a reconciliation statement that explains the differences between the GAAP financial statements and the IFRS financial statements.

IFRS are continually being revised and updated. The International Accounting Standards Board (IASB), which is the body responsible for establishing world wide accounting standards, issues proposals for changes and regular updates. Keeping up with these changes can be a challenge.

Chapter 1 Summary

• GAAP is rules based while IFRS is principles based. IFRS introduces a new way of thinking about financial statements by introducing guidelines rather than strict rules in choosing accounting policies. Judgment decisions will have to be made every day about how to account for financial transactions, deciding on the value of assets, and how to report revenue.

• GAAP measures assets at historical cost while IFRS can measure assets in terms of their potential future benefits.

• "Publicly Accountable Enterprises" must comply. These are companies that "hold assets in a fiduciary capacity", in other words, companies that hold public money "in trust".

• The deadline for comparative IFRS financial statements for "Publicly Accountable Enterprises" in the USA is January 1, 2014 and January 1, 2011 in Canada.

The Four Key Principles

2

Four key principles, clarity, relevance, reliability, and comparability, are the foundation of IFRS. They provide the necessary guidelines for accountants who must make many more judgment decisions under principles based IFRS than they ever did under rules based GAAP.

1) Clarity

The principle of clarity simply means that the financial statements must be easy to read and easy to understand.

Making financial statements understandable to accountants is not a problem. However, not everyone who reads the financial statements is a trained accountant. In fact, most readers are not fluent in accounting jargon. The real challenge is in making the financial statements, especially the notes to the statements, easy for all readers to understand.

To achieve clarity, accountants should choose simplicity over complexity. The true financial position of the company should be clear to anyone.

2) Relevance

IFRS says that an item is relevant if the information about that item has the potential to influence the decisions of lenders, investors, and other users of the financial statements.

The IFRS principle of relevance corresponds to the GAAP principle of materiality. Although in the past, many accountants and audit firms used a specific dollar amount as a minimum guideline to determine if something was material, now more and more accountants are following a standard very close to IFRS which means that they examine the nature of the item as well as the dollar value.

Under the GAAP materiality principle any information which could influence the decisions of lenders, investors, and other users of the statements, should be included at least in the notes, if not in the body of the financial statements.

The IFRS requirement that only relevant information be included means that the accountant must also decide the level of detail. Given that IFRS also demands clarity, the notes to the financial statements must be capable of being understood by the users of the financial statements and add value to the financial statements by adding clarity, and not simply add confusion.

Accountants must be skilled communicators providing relevant, clear, concise notes to the financial statements.

Accountants must be prepared to meet the challenge of defending their decisions concerning relevance to management and the auditor. This is an issue that worries many accountants.

3) Reliability

The principle of reliability refers to the extent to which information presented in the financial statements can be counted on to be true.

True and fair

Reliable information means that the financial statements are a reflection of the company's economic reality. In other words, are they a true and fair presentation of the company's operating results and its financial condition? But what is "true and fair"? In an IFRS context, "true" means that the information is objective and represented in an unbiased manner and "fair" means that common sense prevails because IFRS encourages balancing the level of spending on preparing the statements with the level of value delivered to the readers of the statements. For example, if you have sufficient information, IFRS lets you assign a percentage increase in the aggregate value of a large group of similar assets without the added expense of calculating and verifying the increase for each asset in the group.

Free of material errors

In order for information to be reliable, it must be free of material errors. So just what is material? Material items are those that have the potential to change the opinion of the readers of the financial statements. Materiality is more than just a minimum dollar level. $1000 might be material in one company but not in another, but if the $1000 item involves fraud then it is material to all companies, therefore the nature of the item, not just its dollar value determines materiality. Material information must not be withheld from lenders and creditors. If there is any doubt about whether an item is material or not, the information should be provided. Full disclosure is always the wiser choice.

Neutral

Reliable information must also be neutral. It must be free from bias. Although it is impossible because of human nature to completely eliminate all bias, accountants must continually endeavor to be independent. The notes to the financial statements should be carefully written in a manner that conveys the facts without expressing any personal views or emotions.

Complete

Reliable information must also be complete. One of the goals of IFRS is to inspire confidence that all pertinent information is included.

Substance over form

Decisions about whether information about individual transactions should be reported must be based on the intention of presenting a true and fair picture of the company's results and financial condition. IFRS is very clear that reflecting the company's economic reality in its financial statements is a matter of substance over form.

Prudence

International Financial Reporting Standards requires that accountants who prepare financial statements must exercise judgment in dealing with the inevitable uncertainties of valuation and materiality. They are expected to use a degree of caution in making these judgments. Accountants must be prudent in their approach by considering all the facts and information, both objective and subjective, to produce financial statements that meet the reliability requirement of IFRS.

4) Comparability

The principle of comparability refers to the ability to compare financial statements from year-to-year, company-to-company, and industry-to-industry.

IFRS requires that financial statements focus primarily on the needs of the users of the financial statements rather than the desires of those producing the statements. Comparability is one feature that definitely benefits the end user. Being able to easily compare financial statements is such a desirable factor that it is the driving force behind developing universal standards that enhance comparability. One of the International Accounting Standards Board's objectives is to remove as many choices of accounting methods as possible first within IFRS, then between IFRS and GAAP (both USA and Canadian GAAP), in order to produce a single set of international standards that vary as little as possible from company to company, and from country to country.

However, some accountants have argued that the

emphasis on uniformity of accounting methods to achieve comparability will not produce the most faithful financial statements because it takes away any allowance for differences among individual companies. This group is quickly becoming a minority. Comparability has clearly been recognized as a priority by the accounting profession and demanded by investors.

Trading off

IFRS encourages "trading off" between principles. For example, if information about a particular item is not as reliable as the accountant would like, he or she should add clarity by providing helpful information in expanded notes to the statement. In other words, reduced reliability is exchanged for clarity. This can be applied to any of the four basic principles of IFRS. "Substance over form" demands that a "true and fair" financial statement be presented by the company.

As you can see, being principles based rather than rules based, IFRS allows substantial discretion in deciding what information will be included and how it will be presented or disclosed, the final decision rests with the accountant. This is the aspect of IFRS that makes many accountants uncomfortable, preferring the sense of security that came with being able to follow the old GAAP rules.

Chapter 2 Summary

• International Financial Reporting Standards are governed by four key principles: clarity, relevance, reliability, and comparability.

• The principle of "clarity" simply means that the financial statements must be easy to read and easy to understand.

• An item is "relevant" if the information about that item has the potential to influence the decisions of users of the financial statements.

• "Reliability" refers to the extent to which information presented in the financial statements can be counted on to be true.

• "Comparability" refers to the ability to compare financial statements from year-to-year, company-to-company, and industry-to-industry.

• IFRS allows substantial discretion in deciding what information will be included and how it will be presented or disclosed, the final decision rests with the accountant.

"The company accountant is shy and retiring. He's shy a quarter of a million dollars. That's why he's retiring."

Milton Berle

The Balance Sheet or Statement of Financial Position

3

The balance sheet is the company's list of things it has (assets), money it owes (liabilities), and what the difference is (equity). Under IFRS the balance sheet is called the statement of financial position. The balance sheet is the foundation for the other parts of the financial statements such as the income statement and the cash flow statement. It is the "score" at the end of the accounting reporting period. It compares the current score with the score at the end of the last accounting period. That it why is it is called a comparative statement of financial position. Some companies present three years for comparison even though they are not required to do so under IFRS.

Items are separated into current items (assets and liabilities which are expected to be used up or paid in the next year) and non-current items (assets which will take more than a year to be used up or liabilities that will be paid over a period longer than a year). Within each category they are listed in order of liquidity, which means the ease with which the asset can be sold and converted to cash.

1. Current Assets

Cash and cash equivalents

Cash is classified as a financial asset. It includes cash on hand and demand deposits with banks and other financial institutions which management intends to spend for current purposes (within a year).

Cash which is restricted and not available for use within one year should be included in noncurrent assets, not current assets. An example of this would be a bank loan that requires that a minimum amount of cash (often called a "compensating balance") remain on hand at all times in the company's bank account. The minimum deposit amount is not available for the company to spend. Not only is this a form of collateral for the loan, it increases the effective yield on the loan. IFRS requires a separate disclosure with regard to this cash which is not available for immediate use.

Cash equivalents, also classified as financial assets, include short-term, easy-to-sell investments that can be sold for a predictable amount of cash. To be included in this category, cash equivalents must be free of any significant risk of changes in value. Examples of these are treasury bills and money market funds. In the past, this category would have included commercial paper, but the latest subprime mortgage "credit crunch" proves that some commercial paper can be extremely volatile. Therefore, subprime mortgage commercial paper should be classified as a financial instrument with significant impairment, rather than a cash equivalent.

Inventory

For most companies inventory is one of the largest assets. From an accounting point of view inventory is important because it affects both the income statement and the balance sheet.

Inventory includes items available for sale in the ordinary course of business, as well as materials and supplies used in the manufacturing process or in the rendering of services.

Valuation

Under IFRS inventory must be valued at the lower of cost or net realizable value. Net realizable value is the usual selling price less the estimated selling costs and the costs of making the product available for sale.

FIFO (first-in-first-out) and "weighted average" are the only two acceptable costing methods under IFRS. LIFO used under US GAAP is not acceptable.

Write-downs

Any write-downs of inventory are recorded as an expense in the accounting period in which they occur. If these write-downs or losses, in whole or in part, later reverse themselves, they must be recorded as a reduction of the expense in the accounting period in which the reversal occurs.

Exclusions

IFRS requires that research costs and development costs not be included in inventory costs. R & D costs are expensed in the accounting period in which they occur. Exclusions include administrative and selling expenses, wasted materials, and storage costs.

Accounts receivable

Trade receivables

Accounts receivable include trade receivables for goods and services provided to customers in the normal course of business. As with GAAP, under IFRS, accounts receivable must be reported at net realizable value (an estimate of how much cash will be collected).

How you treat unearned interest and finance charges is optional under GAAP, but they must be deducted under IFRS. In addition, if material, an amount for estimated returns, allowances, and other discounts should be deducted.

Other receivables

Other receivables should be listed in a separate category. Examples of other receivables include notes receivable, and amounts due from related parties, such as officers of the company and associated companies. Under IFRS, these receivables are usually shown separately in their own receivables category, which helps highlight non-trade receivables such as loans to officers.

Pledging accounts receivable

As with GAAP, if accounts receivable are pledged as collateral, no accounting entry is needed, but adequate disclosure in the notes is required.

Assigning accounts receivable

If accounts receivable are assigned to a third party, the assigning company receives a reduced advance payment in return for handing over the rights to collect the customer accounts. Because the accounts receivable are still the assets of the assignor, they continue to be shown in the assigning company's balance sheet along with the appropriate disclosure.

Accounts receivable can be sold outright to a factor without recourse (the factor cannot turn to the selling company for compensation if the accounts receivable become uncollectible) or with recourse (the factor can ask the company to reimburse any bad debt losses). If the risks and rewards associated with the accounts receivable are substantially transferred from the company to the factor, then the asset moves off the company's balance sheet to that of the factor. Otherwise, the company keeps the accounts receivable on its balance sheet and discloses whether they are factored with or without recourse.

Financial Instruments

Under IFRS, a financial instrument is a contract to create a financial asset for one company and a financial liability or equity item for another company. Until the contract is signed neither company should record the financial instrument on its books. The company that records financial liability cannot remove this debt from its books until it has met all the conditions to discharge its debt, or if the instrument expires or is canceled.

Stocks, bonds, and derivatives such as options, forwards, and swaps, are examples of financial instruments. Physical assets, such as inventory, plant and equipment, and intangible assets, such as patents and goodwill, are not considered to be financial instruments.

Unlike GAAP, a commodity future to deliver physical assets, such as pork futures, is also not considered a financial instrument, because the fair value of these physical, non-financial assets cannot be measured reliably until the delivery date.

Classification

Financial assets are classified into 4 groups: 1) Financial assets at fair value (such as cash), 2) Loans and receivables (such as accounts receivable and payable), 3) Held-to-maturity investments which management does not intend to sell (such as certificates of deposit), and 4) Available-for-sale financial assets which management intends to sell (such as stock market shares of public companies).

IAS 39 applies to all financial instruments, except interests in subsidiaries (IAS 27), associates (IAS 28), joint ventures (IAS 31), and leases (IAS 17).

Initial recording

As under GAAP, financial instruments are recorded initially at fair value. Fair value is the amount for which the asset could be exchanged or for which the liability could be settled between two well-informed, willing parties at arm's length. Costs which are directly related to the acquisition of the assets or the incurring of the liability are also added to the fair value when first recorded.

Composite financial instruments

Financial instruments that have both debt and equity components have been a particular challenge with regard to how these items should be presented on the balance sheet. Should they be classified as debt or as equity investments? IAS 39 states that a financial instrument should be classified based on the arrangement contained in the contract. For example, if the contract stipulates that the issuer must provide cash or other financial assets in the future, then it should be classified as a liability, not as an equity instrument.

Impairment

Impairment refers to the change in value, up or down, of an asset from its predicted value. This includes assessing the collectability of financial assets, something which IFRS requires to be reviewed a minimum of once a year. For example, if the anticipated cash flow from a particular financial instrument comes into question for whatever reason, the book value is adjusted downward using the impairment account, along with a corresponding profit or loss on the income statement.

"Derecognition" of financial assets and liabilities

"Derocognition" of a financial asset means that it is taken off the books, or written off. A financial instrument is "derecognized" when the rights to the cash flows or financial asset are transferred. If the rights to the cash flows are kept, but the company assumes an obligation to pay out those cash flows to a third party then that asset will not produce any future cash flows that the company can use. Since IFRS says that an asset is measured in terms of its expected future cash flows, then the value of an asset that does not produce cash flows is zero and must be removed from the balance sheet or "derecognized".

The amount of the transfer will depend on the extent to which the risks and rewards of ownership are passed on. Whoever ends up with most of the risks and rewards must keep the asset or liability on their books. If ownership is difficult to determine, then the level of control over the asset or liability and the level of risk of loss become the determining factors. IAS 39 defines control simply as the company's right to sell the asset or settle the liability.

Partial derecognition

A financial instrument is "derecognized" in part when that part of the financial instrument has its own separate identifiable cash flows, such as interest. The extent to which the instrument is "derecognized" is in proportion to the total value of the instrument. For example, if interest is 10% of the value of an instrument then 90% remains on the balance sheet.

Hedge accounting

IAS 39 talks about 3 types of hedging relationships: fair value hedges, cash flow hedges, and hedges of net investment in a foreign company.

A fair value hedge covers the risk that the value of the asset or liability might change and produce a negative effect on profit. A cash flow hedge, usually a derivative or other financial instrument, covers the risk that the asset's cash flow will not be received as predicted. A hedge of net investment in a foreign company is a financial instrument that protects the company from the risks associated with dealing with other countries, for example, from the risk of loss due to political instability, or currency fluctuations.

If all financial instruments could be "marked to market values," there would be little need for hedge accounting. Hedge accounting requires formal documentation that spells out the hedging relationship between the financial asset and the hedging instrument. In addition, hedge accounting assumes that hedging will be effective in offsetting changes in the fair value of the financial asset and throughout the financial reporting period. It also assumes that this effectiveness can be measured reliably.

Substance over form

Compared to US GAAP, IFRS promotes a "substance over form" approach to establishing the classification and assignment of value for financial instruments. In other words, it is more important that the reader be able to clearly understand the financial situation (the substance) rather than simply following a standard set of presentation guidelines (the form). In order to do this effectively the accountant must examine the contract and really understand the nature of a particular financial instrument in order to decide how it should be classified and what valued should be assigned to it.

IAS 39 also provides guidelines for the impairment of available-for-sale investments. Available-for-sale refers to an investment that has been purchased with the intention of reselling it, versus something that has been purchased as a permanent investment. Impairment losses on available-for-sale equity instruments cannot be reversed through profit or loss. In other words, once there has been an impairment decrease in value recorded as a loss, any reversal should be recorded as an increase in equity and not as profit. This prevents the kind of manipulation prevalent during the high tech bubble of the 1990's where companies would adjust the values of financial instruments in order to manipulate the stock price.

Disclosure

IFRS 7 requires that companies disclose exactly how important financial instruments are to the company's financial position and performance.

Specifically, companies need to describe the nature and extent of the risks associated with each class of financial instruments such as credit risk, liquidity risk, and market risk.

This IFRS 7 disclosure requirement applies to all

companies that have financial instruments, even if the only "financial instruments" they have are accounts receivable and accounts payable.

"Trading securities"

"Trading securities" are public traded company shares and derivatives acquired with the intent of earning a profit in the short-term by taking advantage of anticipated price fluctuations. These include debt and equity securities, loans and receivables. Because the prices of these securities fluctuate regularly, changes in the value are reported in the income statement of the current reporting period. In addition, IAS 39 calls for derivatives to be classified as held-for-trading unless they are held for hedging purposes only.

Prepaid expenses

Prepaid expenses are assets produced by the prepayment of cash or by incurring a liability. Over time they expire and become expenses, such as prepaid rent. They also can become expenses when they are used, such as deferred taxes. Prepaid expenses are usually lumped together as a single amount on the balance sheet. The individual amounts are usually not material enough to warrant separate disclosure.

2. <u>Noncurrent assets</u>

Held-to-maturity investments

According to IAS 39, held-to-maturity investments are non-derivative financial assets with fixed payments and fixed maturity which the enterprise intends (and can afford) to hold to maturity. This can include debt securities of other companies such as bonds. However, this does not include loans and receivables issued by the enterprise, which are classified separately. Held-to-maturity investments are measured at cost.

Change of intent

If there is a change of intent (often associated with a change in management) or the enterprise becomes unable to continue to hold the asset to maturity because it needs the cash immediately, then they must be reclassified as available-for-sale. This would also bring into question the possible reclassification of all held-to-maturity investments. IAS 39 prohibits the subsequent reversal of these reclassifications of financial instruments to prevent "cherry picking" and manipulation of fair values (and the income statement) through the impairment account.

Lack of market price

Unless there is impairment in value, held-to-maturity investments must be recorded and maintained at historical cost (amortized using the effective interest rate method). This also applies to any financial asset which does not have a quoted price in an active market because its fair value cannot be measured reliably.

Investment property

Investment property is property that is either held to earn rental income or is held with the intention of being sold at a profit later. It is not property intended to be used in the course of the company's normal business (such as a building which contains the company's offices). It must be probable that economic benefits will flow from the investment to the company in the future and that this estimated cash flow can be measured reliably. An investment property must be initially recorded at cost (including transaction costs).

Leases

IAS 40 says that "a property interest that is held by a lessee under an operating lease may be classified and accounted for as investment property." In other words, an operating lease is treated as if it were a finance lease. As in many other areas, IFRS requires that the fair value of investment property is the price at which the property "could be exchanged between knowledgeable, willing parties in an arm's length transaction."

Disposal

An investment property is "derecognized" (taken off the balance sheet) when it is sold or withdrawn from use and no future economic benefits are expected. Gains and losses on retirement or disposal of investment property are included in the income statement.

Property, Plant, and Equipment

Property, Plant, and Equipment are long-term tangible assets (fixed assets) used in the production or supply of goods or services. In addition, it includes space used for its own administrative purposes as well as assets rented to another entity during more than one accounting period. Examples include land, buildings, furniture, fixtures, and equipment. Again, it must be probable that economic benefits will flow from the investment to the company in the future and that this estimated cash flow can be measured reliably.

Initial cost

A property, plant and equipment asset is measured at its cost. Cost includes the cash price, import duties and non-refundable purchase taxes, delivery and preparation, while deducting trade discounts and rebates.

If payment is on normal credit terms, the interest is an expense over the period of credit. However, if interest is first incurred to make the asset available for use (for example when the company borrows to construct its own building) it is included in the carrying amount of the asset.

Valuation choices

After the initial recording of a property, plant and equipment asset, the enterprise can choose either the cost model or the revaluation model as its accounting policy which must be applied to the entire class of property, plant and equipment to which that particular asset belongs.

Cost model

If the company chooses to apply the cost model to an item in a class of property, plant and equipment assets, then that asset is carried at its cost less any accumulated depreciation and any accumulated impairment losses.

Revaluation model

If the company chooses to apply the revaluation model to an item in a class of property, plant and equipment assets whose fair value can be measured reliably, then that asset is carried at a revalued amount which is its fair value at the date of the revaluation (usually the end of the reporting period) less any subsequent accumulated depreciation and subsequent accumulated impairment losses.

If a property, plant and equipment asset's carrying amount is increased as a result of a revaluation, the increase is first used to reverse any previous revaluation decrease of the same asset. The rest of the increase, if any, is recorded in other "comprehensive income" and accumulated in equity as "revaluation surplus."

If a property, plant and equipment asset's carrying amount is decreased as a result of a revaluation, the decrease is applied to any credit balance related to that asset already existing in the revaluation surplus account. The rest of the decrease is then recorded as a "comprehensive loss".

Cash generating units

A cash generating unit is the smallest identifiable group of assets that generates independent and reliably measurable cash inflows. Some examples of possible cash generating units include departments, production lines, or a factory.

By requiring that the grouping be made at the lowest possible level, IAS 36 tries to prevent the offsetting of impairments which might make the impairment easier to hide in a larger group of assets.

IAS 36 requires a consistent approach to defining cash generating units from one accounting period to the next. In addition, the discount rate should be the same one used for all impairment testing at any given date. Of course, the discount rate must also be adjusted to reflect the risk associated with a particular asset.

Impairment of property, plant and equipment assets

IFRS requires that assets must be carried at no more than their recoverable amount. If an asset's carrying amount is greater than its fair value, the asset is deemed to be impaired. The fair value of the asset used for this comparison is the lower of either what the asset is worth to the company by using it or its market value if the company were to sell the asset. The carrying amount is reduced to the recoverable amount and an impairment loss is recorded.

Impairment of tangible long-lived assets can occur as a result of natural disasters, such as floods and hurricanes. When payment from third parties, such as insurance companies, is received to compensate for some of the loss, the payments are not netted for financial reporting purposes.

Disclosure

As under GAAP, the amounts net of depreciation should be shown on the balance sheet. In the notes to the financial statements, the expected useful life, cost, accumulated depreciation, and the method used to calculate depreciation, should be listed by major class.

If impairment loss is increased or reversed during the accounting period, the notes to the financial statements should disclose the nature, cause and the amount of the loss or reversal, a description of the particular asset or cash-generating unit, additions and disposals, and how the recoverable amount was calculated (value in use or market price) including the discount rate.

Intangible assets

IAS 38 defines an intangible asset as "an identifiable non-monetary asset without physical substance." While a building is an example of a long-lived tangible asset, a copyright is an example of an intangible long-lived asset.

To add an intangible asset to the balance sheet, it must be identifiable and its value must be reliably measurable.

Identifiable

An intangible asset is "identifiable" if the company has the right to sell it as a separate asset. It can also be "identifiable" if it is possible to sell the contractual or other legal rights to the asset.

Valuation

A separately acquired intangible asset (not goodwill) is initially recorded at cost which includes purchase price and the cost of getting the asset ready for its intended use.

After the initial recording of the intangible asset, the enterprise can choose either the cost model or the revaluation model as its accounting policy (this must be applied to the entire class.)

Cost model

If the company chooses to apply the cost model to an intangible asset, then that asset is carried at its cost less any accumulated amortization and any accumulated impairment losses.

Revaluation model

As with tangible assets, if the company chooses to apply the revaluation model to an item in a class of intangible assets, then all the assets in that class must be revalued to their fair value. Fair value is the price in an active market when the items traded are all the same, there are willing buyers and sellers, and the same prices are available to anyone.

The treatment of increases or decreases in the value of intangible assets as a result of revaluation is the same as that of long-lived tangible assets.

The residual value of an intangible asset with a limited useful life is assumed to be zero unless there is an amount recoverable from the sale of the intangible asset at the end of its useful life or there is an active market for the asset which provides a reliable end-of-life price.

The useful life estimate and related amortization period must be reviewed every year. An intangible asset with an indefinite useful life is not amortized and must be tested for impairment at least every year.

Exclusions

IAS 38 specifically excludes internally generated brands, mastheads, publishing titles, customer lists and items similar in substance from being recorded on the balance sheet as intangible assets.

Research and development

Research costs are not recorded as an asset. They are recorded as an expense when they are incurred. Development costs may be recorded at cost as an intangible asset if all of the following conditions are met:

- It is technically feasible to complete making the intangible asset available for use or sale.

- The company intends and has the ability to use or sell the intangible asset once it is completed.

- The company can demonstrate probable future economic benefits and a use or market for the intangible asset.

- The company has access to enough technical, financial and other resources to complete the development and to use or sell the intangible asset.

- The company can measure reliably the costs related to the development of the intangible asset.

Development costs that do not qualify cannot be expensed. The recording of these costs cannot be reversed later to record them as an intangible asset.

Goodwill

When a business pays more than the value of the assets of another business, there is an assumption that the premium itself has value. This difference between the price paid and the fair value of the assets is recorded as acquired goodwill. Every year, the value of acquired goodwill should be tested to see if it has been impaired. If yes, it must be written down. It cannot be reversed if it goes up later as acquired goodwill is gradually replaced by internally generated goodwill. Internally generated goodwill is not recorded as an asset.

Disclosure

The values of intangible assets should be listed net of amortization on the balance sheet. In the notes to the financial statements, the expected useful life, cost, accumulated amortization, and the method used to calculate amortization, should be shown by major class. Examples of possible classes include brand names, licenses, intangible assets under development, computer software, and copyrights.

If impairment loss is increased or reversed during the accounting period, the notes to the financial statements should disclose the nature, cause and the amount of the loss or reversal, a description of the particular intangible asset, additions and disposals, and how the recoverable amount was calculated (value in use or market price) including the amortization rate.

Assets "held for sale"

IFRS 5 requires that a non-current asset be classified as "held-for-sale". This class can also be referred to as a "disposal group", if the investment in this asset will be recovered by selling it instead of using it up. Specifically, the asset or disposal group must be available for immediate sale at a reasonable price and that there is a high probability of selling as evidenced by a management plan to do so.

"Discontinued operations"

Assets that are classified as "held-for-sale" are often a result of a decision by management to stop part of the company's operations and to sell off the associated assets. A "discontinued operation" is a separate part of the business, or in a separate geographical area. It can also be a subsidiary that was bought with the sole purpose of being resold. The operational and financial reporting structure of the discontinued operation must be clearly separate from the rest of the company.

Abandoned assets

IFRS says that a discontinued operation should not be classified as "held-for-sale" if management plans to abandon it. This is because the asset is not actually for sale.

Other assets

This is an all-inclusive grouping of assets that do not quite fit into any of the other asset categories. Examples are long-term deferred expenses that will not be spent within the next year, such as maintenance contracts. It also includes deferred tax assets that are a result of timing differences. All the impairment and disclosure rules apply to these other assets.

3. Current liabilities

A liability is classified as a current liability if it is due within the current year. If the company intends to trade a liability, regardless of when it is due to be paid, then that liability is classified as a current liability. Debts that are due on demand or callable by the lender at any time, such as bank demand loans, are classified as current liabilities even if management intends to repay these demand loans over a long period of time. All other liabilities are classified as noncurrent liabilities.

Examples of current liabilities include accounts payable, wages payable, taxes payable, and the current portion of any long-term debt. In addition, deposits for undelivered services, such as rent and subscriptions, are current liabilities.

Whether a liability is classified as a current liability or not comes down to whether the company has both the intent and the financial ability to pay the debt within a year.

4. Non-current liabilities

A liability is classified as a non-current liability if it is due and is expected to be paid at a time beyond the current year.

Examples of noncurrent liabilities include bonds, long-term notes payable, and leases longer than a year. In addition, pensions and deferred taxes are classified as non-current liabilities.

If the company is in breach of covenants included in long-term debt agreements that allow the creditor to demand immediate payment, then these debts must be reclassified as current liabilities.

5. Offsetting assets and liabilities

IFRS requires, as a general principle, that assets and liabilities not be offset. However, the reduction of accounts receivable by the amount of the allowance for bad debt is not regarded as an offset. Similarly, property, plant, and equipment reduced by the amount of accumulated depreciation is also not regarded as an offset.

In order to offset assets and liabilities, a contractual right of offset must exist. IFRS requires that any amounts that two parties owe each other must be measured reliably, and that a contract exists which provides a legal right to deduct the amounts due from any amounts owed. In some countries, the bankruptcy and insolvency laws may not allow the offsetting of assets and liabilities.

In the past, financial institutions often offset financial instruments they sold to each other, repackaging them when reselling them. This made it more difficult to discern individual instruments whose quality may be questionable. IFRS has now limited the offsetting of financial instruments.

6. Stockholders' Equity

Share capital

Share capital is the nominal (called "par") value of outstanding common and preferred shares. Some shares may have been issued in the past, but have been purchased back ("redeemed") by the company. As under GAAP, financial statements must state the number of shares authorized, and issued.

Preferred shares may have additional rights attached to them such as receiving dividends before any are distributed to common shareholders, the rights to convert the share to debt, right of redemption by the company, etc.

If the preferred shareholder has the right to demand that the company repurchases the preferred shares at any time, then these preferred shares are classified as a liability, not share capital. Under IFRS, "substance over form" demands that a company's potential obligation be reported as a liability.

Retained earnings

Retained earnings are the accumulated profits that have not been distributed to shareholders in the form of dividends. Some countries have a legal requirement that companies hold back a certain portion of retained earnings as a "reserve."

Other equity items

Some shares may have been repurchased by the company where this is not prevented by law. These shares are listed at acquisition cost in the equity section of the balance sheet as "treasury stock." The amount of the original stock issued continues to be reported on the balance sheet.

Under IFRS, some parts of comprehensive income are added directly to equity without first going through the income statement. An example of such an item is the net change in the value of "available-for-sale" shares of other public companies held in the company's portfolio. These changes are recorded as direct increases or decreases in equity.

Unlike GAAP, minority interests should always be included in the equity section of the balance sheet. They are shown separately from the equity of the parent company.

A subsequent event is an event that occurs between the balance sheet date and the date the financial statements are issued. An example would be the settling of a pending court case. Subsequent events should be disclosed if they affect the estimates used to assign values. These are called "adjusting" events because they cause a change in the way values are estimated. Subsequent events which do not cause changes in values should be disclosed if they have the potential to change an investor's decision.

The company must also disclose if any dividends are proposed or declared after the balance sheet date.

In addition, IAS 1 requires disclosure of the company's legal form, registered legal address, the nature of its business activities, the names of parent companies, and the number of employees at the balance sheet date.

7. <u>Format</u>

Some countries require precise formats for financial statements. Although IFRS does not set out any particular format, they recommend the use of categories if they are relevant.

Under IFRS, a complete set of financial statements for the reporting period (which must be prepared at least on an annual basis) is made up of:

1. **Statement of Financial Position** (Balance Sheet) (beginning and ending)

2. **Statement of Comprehensive Income** (new under IFRS) which includes a Statement of **Results of Operations** (Income Statement)

3. **Statement of Changes in Equity** (Statement of Equity and Retained Earnings)

4. **Statement of Cash Flows** (Statement of Changes in Financial Position)

5. **Notes to the Financial Statements** (which include significant accounting policies and other explanations)

There are many variations of the names of accounts and statements in use in the many countries where IFRS has been adopted. Standardization of these names is an ongoing process.

Chapter 3 Summary

IFRS is changing the way the balance sheet is presented in financial statements in several significant ways:

• The name is changed from "balance sheet" to "statement of financial position".

• IFRS introduces a new way to set asset values by using the present value of expected future benefits or cash flows.

• Assets can be grouped into "cash generating units" in order to more easily assess and record any impairment in the value of the asset group.

• IFRS removes contingent liabilities from the balance sheet.

• Under IFRS, offsetting, except in specifically mentioned areas, is not allowed.

• IFRS financial statements provide readers a clearer picture of the company's current financial position and its ability to generate cash in the future.

An accountant is having a hard time sleeping and goes to see his doctor.

"Doctor, I just can't get to sleep at night."

"Have you tried counting sheep?"

"That's the problem - I make a mistake and then spend three hours trying to find it."

from www.workjoke.com

The Income Statement or Statement of Results of Operations

4

The income statement records the utilization of assets and the fluctuation in liabilities over the accounting period. Under IFRS, the income statement is called the "statement of results of operations". It explains any changes in the balance sheet items from the beginning to the end of the accounting period. It is similar to a "play by play" of a game that describes the change in the score from period to period.

1) Revenue Recognition

What is revenue?

IAS 18 says that revenue is recorded (recognized) when it is probable that future economic benefits will accrue to the business and that these benefits can be measured reliably. For example, a three year, $1 million dollar contract to deliver a service at a cost of $800,000 is immediately recorded as an asset of $1 million, a liability of $800,000, and an equity item of $200,000. The effect of these future economic benefits (in this case, the expected profit of $200,000 which will accrue as revenue over the three years) eventually shows up in the equity section of the financial statements as retained earnings or is distributed as dividends.

"Ordinary" business activities include the sale of goods, the rendering of services, and the use by others of company assets which results in receiving interest, royalties or dividends. It does not include any increases in equity as a result of contributions from shareholders.

Sale of goods

Revenue is recorded when:

- the significant risks and rewards of ownership have been transferred from the seller to the buyer

- the seller no longer has any effective control over the goods

- the amount of revenue can be measured reliably

- the seller determines that they will probably be able to collect the money

- the costs of the transaction can be measured reliably

Rendering of services

When the amount of service revenue can be reliably predicted IFRS requires that you record the revenue based on the stage of completion at the end of the reporting period. This is called the percentage of completion method.

For example, if 60% of the services have been delivered, then 60% of the revenue is recorded if both the stage of completion and the costs to complete the contract can be measured reliably.

When the amount of service revenue cannot be measured reliably, revenue is recorded on the basis of expenses that can be billed to the customer.

Interest, royalties and dividends

Interest revenue recorded is the amount of interest charged to the customer.

Royalties are recorded on an accrual basis based on the agreement between the company and its client.

Dividends are recorded when they are declared by the company.

Exchange of goods or services

If any revenue involves the exchange of goods or services, and the goods or services are similar, then it is not considered revenue. If it is simply an exchange, such as in the swapping of commodities, then no revenue is recorded. For example, if one oil company is short of inventory and "borrows" oil from another company to deliver to its customers, and then returns the same quantity to the lending company later when it replenishes its inventory, neither company records the revenue because it was an exchange of a similar item of equal value. However, if the goods or services exchanged are not similar, then it is considered revenue.

Valuation

IFRS requires that revenue be measured at fair value including any discounts or rebates. IFRS defines fair value as "the amount for which an asset could be exchanged, or a liability settled, between knowledgeable, willing parties in an arm's length transaction."

Disclosures

IFRS requires that the accounting policies used for revenue recognition be disclosed. This includes the method used for determining the stage of completion of service contracts.

The revenue must be broken down for each category of revenue:

- Sale of goods
- Rendering of services
- Interest, royalties and dividends.

2) Cost of Goods Sold

The cost of goods sold is the cost of the inventory which has been sold during the accounting period. The switch from GAAP to IFRS does not change anything in terms of calculating the cost of goods sold.

Distribution

For a distribution company that buys inventory and resells it, the cost of buying the goods including freight (less any allowances, discounts, rebates and returns) is added to the beginning inventory to arrive at the cost of goods available for sale. The ending inventory is deducted from the cost of goods available for sale to calculate the cost of goods sold.

Manufacturing

For a company that manufactures the products it sells instead of buying them, the cost of purchasing the goods is replaced by the cost of making them. The cost of goods manufactured includes raw materials, labor, and a portion of the overhead such as the cost of the manufacturing equipment maintenance costs.

3) Operating expenses

Operating expenses include costs that tend to reoccur every period, such as rent and insurance. They do not include the cost of goods sold.

Under IFRS operating expenses are grouped in two main categories:

- distribution costs (selling expenses) such as sales commissions
- general and administrative expenses, such as office supplies

Other revenues and expenses

Other revenues and expenses are items that are not related to the company's core activity. For example, a company that manufactures electronic parts might rent out part of its building that it does not need for day-to-day operations. The rent revenue and related expenses would be reported as other revenue and expenses in the IFRS financial statements.

4) Income tax expense

IAS 12 says that the tax expense includes all the taxes, both domestic and foreign, payable on the balance sheet date as well as the deferred tax adjustments for the reporting period based on taxable profits, including subsidiaries, associate companies, and joint ventures.

Deferred tax adjustments exist because the rules for preparing financial statements for tax purposes usually are different from IFRS or GAAP. These are usually timing differences that involve the postponement of the payment of taxes to a future accounting period.

Deferred tax liability or asset

Under IFRS, taxes owing for current and prior periods are listed on the balance sheet as a current liability. However, if the company's payments for taxes exceed the amount due for current taxes, then this "prepayment" is an asset on the balance sheet.

Measurement

The amount of taxes is calculated using the tax rates and rules applicable at the balance sheet date. Under IFRS deferred tax assets and deferred tax liabilities are not discounted.

Review

IAS 12 requires a yearly review of deferred tax assets and liabilities. If it is probable that future taxable profit can be reduced by the amount of unused tax losses and unused tax credits that have been carried forward, IFRS requires that the company record a deferred tax asset equal to the expected reduction in taxes. However, if it becomes probable that the company will not have sufficient future taxable profit to be able to use up any part of the deferred tax asset, then the deferred tax asset must be reduced to the level the company believes will probably be used. Of course, if future taxable profit becomes probable again, the reduction of the deferred tax asset must be reversed.

Reporting

IAS 12 stipulates that a company must account for the tax consequences of transactions and events at the same time that the transactions and events themselves are recorded. In other words, the profit or loss recorded in the income statement should also include the tax effect of these transactions and events.

Business combination

Deferred tax assets and liabilities must be taken into account when calculating the amount of goodwill that will be recorded in a business combination.

5) Discontinued operations

IFRS 5 defines a discontinued operation as a "component" of a company that has been disposed of or is in the process of being disposed of. The assets that will be sold with the discontinued operations are listed separately in a new category called "held for sale."

IFRS requires that there be an active management plan to dispose of these assets. These assets usually belong to a separate major line of business or a part of operations in a particular geographical area. A subsidiary acquired exclusively to be resold is also listed in this "held for sale" section. In either case, management must have an active sales plan in place to dispose of these assets.

High probability

IFRS 5 requires that the sale be "highly probable" as evidenced by an active plan to find a buyer who will buy the disposal group under terms that are customary for the industry and conditions in which the company operates. IFRS 5 says that the price must be "reasonable" in relation to the value of the disposal group and that the sale is expected to occur within a year of classifying assets as part of a disposal group and held for sale.

Component

IFRS requires that the operations and cash flows of this "discontinued" component of the company be separate, both operationally and for financial reporting, from the rest of the company. In other words, a discontinued operations component will have been a self-contained cash-generating unit or a group of cash-generating units while being held for use.

Abandoning assets

If a company intends to abandon a long-term asset when the operations are discontinued instead of selling it, then the company cannot classify it as "held for sale." The write-down must be included in the discontinued operations section of comprehensive income. IFRS assumes that the value (carrying amount) of the asset will be recovered by using it.

Valuation

IFRS 5 says that assets held for sale are valued at the lower of carrying amount and fair value less costs to sell, net of tax. It requires that depreciation on the assets of discontinued operations stop.

Presentation

IFRS 5 stipulates that assets of discontinued operations which are classified as held for sale must be presented separately in the balance sheet. These assets, which are to be sold as a group, are called a "disposal group." The results of discontinued operations also must be presented separately in the statement of comprehensive income.

6) Gains and losses

Unfortunately, IFRS do not provide any guidelines for separating gains and losses from income and expenses. Interestingly, the IASB has stipulated that gains and losses are essentially the same as income and expenses because they describe the same thing: an increase or decrease in economic benefits for the company. However, current practice is to classify the result of items that may be beyond a company's control (gains and losses) as operating or non-operating.

7) Statement of changes in equity

IAS 1 requires that a company include a statement of changes in equity in its financial statements. The statement of changes in equity will show:

- the net profit or loss for the period
- gains and losses
- the effects of changes in accounting policies
- corrections of errors
- related party capital transactions
- changes in the retained earnings
- changes in each class of shares

IAS 19 allows companies to present a statement of recorded income and expenses, which outlines all changes in actuarial gains and losses of defined benefit pension plans.

Dividends distributed to shareholders during the period, both as a total and as an amount per share, should be included in the face of the statement of changes in equity or in the notes to the financial statements.

8) Format

The format under IFRS is essentially the same as under GAAP. The first line of the income statement is the legal name of the company and the next line is the accounting period which is covered by the income statement.

The income statement headings include:

- revenue
- finance costs
- profits and losses related to associates and joint ventures
- tax expense
- discontinued operations
- profit or loss
- minority interests
- net profit belonging to shareholders in the parent company

The IFRS directive of substance over form dictates that the format should be adjusted if the changes add clarity, relevance, reliability, or comparability. However, IFRS does not permit grouping items together, including offsetting revenue and expense items, in order to hide important information.

Chapter 4 Summary

• IFRS refers to the "income statement" as the "statement of results of operations".

• Revenue is recorded (recognized) when it is probable that future economic benefits will accrue to the business and that these benefits can be measured reliably.

• Service revenue is recorded based on the stage of completion at the end of the reporting period and must be measured at fair value including any discounts or rebates allowed by the company.

• Accounting policies used for revenue recognition are to be disclosed.

• Taxes owing for current and prior periods are listed on the balance sheet as a current liability and IAS 12 requires a yearly review of deferred tax assets and liabilities.

• Assets of discontinued operations which are classified as held for sale must be presented separately in the balance sheet, valued at the lower of carrying amount and fair value less costs to sell, net of tax, and that there be an active management plan to dispose of the assets.

Cash Flow Statement

5

The cash flow statement explains the change in the cash balance from the beginning of the period to the end of the period. It shows where the company gets its cash, and where it spends it. Because the income statement measures accounting profit, the cash flow statement removes the effect of accounting entries that do not affect cash, such as depreciation and deferral of taxes.

1) Cash flows

IAS 7 stipulates that a company must include a statement of cash flows in its financial statements. The statement of cash flows tells the reader how much cash the company has, where the company got its cash, and how it spent it.

What a company does with its cash tells investors and lenders how well it is able to pay its bills and meet its other financial commitments as they fall due. In other words, it describes the firm's ability to generate cash as needed. The timing and the certainty of cash generation is a vital part of assessing a company's ability to not only to survive in the short-term, but also to thrive in the long-term.

What are cash flows?

IFRS defines cash flows as "flows of cash and cash equivalents." "Cash" is simply the cash on hand, such as the amount in the bank account. "Cash equivalents" are short-term investments that can be easily exchanged for cash whose value is not likely to change.

The statement of cash flows separates cash flows during the period by classifying them into operating (day-to-day business), financing (borrowing), and investing (spending) activities.

Operating activities

Operating activities are the day-to-day business transactions that produce revenue for the company. The amount of cash as a result of operating activities is a key indicator of the company's ability to pay all the things it has to pay, such as payroll, bank loans, suppliers, and dividends, without resorting to borrowing any money from the bank or other lenders.

Under IFRS, a company can choose to report cash flows from operating activities in one of three ways:

- The direct method
- The indirect method
- The modified indirect method

1. Direct method

IFRS permits a company to use the "direct method" of reporting cash flows from operating activities. This means that gross cash receipts and gross cash payments are classified into major classes, such as payments from customers, interest and dividends received, cash paid to employees and suppliers, interest paid, income taxes paid, and other operating cash receipts and payments. Although this method requires more meticulous bookkeeping, a company that receives most of its revenue in cash might choose this method.

2. Indirect method

IFRS also allows a firm to use the "indirect method" (often called the reconciliation method) of reporting cash flows from operating activities. Under this method, the profit or loss is adjusted for non-cash transactions such as depreciation and amortization, and for any "deferrals or accruals of past or future operating cash receipts or payments" such as deferred taxes. Although IFRS encourages the direct method, the indirect method is the most commonly used because it is easier to complete.

3. Modified indirect method

IAS 7 offers a third method, not available under GAAP, called the "modified indirect method" to report cash flows from operating activities. This adaptation of the indirect method only differs from the indirect method in that it begins with revenue and expenses as reported on the income statement instead of starting with net income. A company might choose this method if it prefers to provide more details about the revenue and expenses rather than use only the net income amount.

Financing activities

Financing activities are transactions that change the equity and debt sections of the company's balance sheet. In other words, other than operating activities, the company gets its cash from lenders (debt) and from investors (shareholder equity). Understanding the effect of financing activities on cash flows helps readers of the financial statements understand what demands lenders and investors could make on the company's cash flow in the future.

Financing transactions that do not call for the use of cash or cash equivalents are not included in the statement of cash flows. However, they must be disclosed in the notes to the financial statements.

Investing activities

Investing activities are the acquisition and disposal of long-term assets and other investments not included in cash equivalents. This section of the cash flow statement shows how the company has spent money buying and selling assets in the hope of generating future income and cash flows. IAS 7 requires that the effect on cash flows of buying or selling subsidiaries or other businesses must be presented separately and classified as investing activities.

2) Netting out cash flows

As noted previously, IAS 7 requires that cash receipts and disbursements be listed in gross amounts on the statement of cash flows. IFRS generally does not permit the netting out of cash receipts and cash disbursements. For example, if notes payable were issued and then paid all within the same accounting period, both the issuance and payment of the notes payable would be disclosed separately and the effect on cash would not be netted out.

One exception allowed by IAS 7 is netting out cash flows of items with quick turnovers, large amounts, and short maturities, such as 10-day notes, and the other is netting out cash flows that are a result of customer activity rather than the activity of the company.

3) Foreign currency

IAS 7 stipulates that foreign currency transactions are to be recorded in the company's reporting currency using the exchange rate in effect on the date of the transaction. Cash flows from foreign operations are reported in a separate statement using the exchange rate in effect on the date of the transactions, which is then rolled up into the consolidated cash flow statement.

The effect of fluctuations in the exchange rate on cash and cash equivalents held or due in a foreign currency is reported in the statement of cash flows. This allows the company to reconcile cash and cash equivalents at the beginning and the end of the period.

4) Extraordinary items

GAAP allows but does not require separate disclosure of cash flows linked to extraordinary items. IAS 1 however takes away this option and requires that gains and losses from extraordinary items be reported separately in IFRS compliant statements. In other words, the company must list extraordinary gains separately from the extraordinary losses on the statement of income.

5) Acquisitions and disposals

IAS 7 stipulates that the cash flows related to acquisitions and disposals of subsidiaries and other business units be disclosed separately as part of investing activities in the cash flow statement.

6) Required disclosures

IAS 7 requires that the company disclose, along with a commentary by management, the amount of significant cash and cash equivalent balances held by the company that are not available for use. For example, if the company has obtained a $1 million bank loan on condition that the company keeps at least $100,000 on deposit at the bank, then the company must disclose that the $100,000 is not available for use.

7) Recommended disclosures

IAS 7 recommends, but does not require, the following disclosures which may help the reader of the financial statements better understand the company's cash position:

Unused borrowing facilities

The company may disclose the amount of unused credit lines along with applicable restrictions that apply to those credit lines.

Cash flow related to maintaining production capacity

This is the amount of cash needed to maintain the level of production capacity as separate from the cash required to increase production capacity.

Segment reporting

In addition to the consolidated cash flow statement, the company may choose to report cash flows separately by business segment or geographical region.

The importance of the cash flow statement

The statement of cash flows is critical for the readers of the company's financial statements. Investors want to know if the company has enough money to carry out its plans and meet its financial goals. Lenders and investors want to know if they will get their money back. Even employees will look to the cash flow statement to see if the company can afford to pay the bonuses it has promised. The cash flow statement is therefore an indicator of the company's ability to generate enough cash to sustain it in the long-term and keep its investors and lenders happy to continue providing cash to the company.

Chapter 5 Summary

• IAS 7: a statement of cash flows must be included in the financial statements. IFRS defines cash flows as flows of cash and cash equivalents.

• Cash flows from operating activities must be recorded in

one of three ways:
- The direct method
- The indirect method
- The modified indirect method

- Financing activities are transactions that change the equity and debt sections of the company's balance sheet.

- Investing activities are the acquisition and disposal of long-term assets and other investments not included in cash equivalents.

- IFRS generally does not permit the netting out of cash receipts and cash disbursements.

- Foreign currency transactions are to be recorded in the company's reporting currency using the exchange rate in effect on the date of the transactions.

- Extraordinary gains must be listed separately from extraordinary losses on the statement of income (they cannot be netted out against each other).
- Required disclosures:
  - Unused borrowing facilities
  - Cash flow related to maintaining production capacity

Disclosures

6

Although GAAP required a number of disclosures, IFRS requires even more. The disclosures that are part of the financial statements provide explanations to the investor about how the company calculated the items reported. In addition, they are intended to make the investor confident that the financial statements are reliable. If the notes are not clear, reliable, and relevant, the investor might decide to move their money to a company where the financial statements are easier to understand.

1) Explanations

Disclosures are the explanations that help the readers better understand the financial statements. They may not only provide information as to how a particular asset was valued, but in addition may express an opinion as to the extent to which that method may be relied upon.

Although many disclosures are mandatory, IFRS also demands the inclusion of any disclosure that helps the user of the financial statements.

If the supplemental information is only a few words, it can be added in parentheses next to the item in the financial statements.

Sometimes, the extra information can also be in a footnote if it is too long to fit in a single line, but too short to warrant a full note to the financial statement.

2) Accounting policies

A note is required under IFRS that explains the method of accounting the company used. Not only should the overall accounting method be disclosed, but the choice of accounting policies in specific areas, such as revenue recognition policies and depreciation policies must be disclosed.

If the company makes a voluntary change in accounting policy, it must disclose the nature and reason for the change. In addition, it must disclose the effect this change has on the financial statement. These changes include those that affect the current year as well as the effect on future financial statements. An example would be a change in policy regarding how the company records the value of its inventory.

If the company decides to apply a new IFRS standard that has been issued but not yet in effect, the company must disclose this fact and the impact of this decision on the financial statement.

A change in accounting estimate, such as a change in the amount of ore estimated to be remaining in a silver mine, must be disclosed along with the effect this change has on the financial statement.

If prior period adjustments must be made, IFRS requires disclosure of the nature, amount, and reason for the adjustment. In addition the affect of the adjustment, now and in the future, must be disclosed.

If it is not possible to estimate reliably the future effects of any of the changes in accounting policies or accounting estimates, then the company must disclose that fact to the readers of the financial statements.

3) Exception: IFRS #1

IFRS #1 is the standard that applies when a company adopts IFRS for the first time. This Standard allows exceptions to IFRS rules in the first year only to help companies with the transition from GAAP to IFRS.

IFRS allows a company to make an exception by not applying a particular IFRS standard if the company believes that a less misleading statement will be the result of not following the particular standard.

IFRS 1 requires that the company disclose:

• Management's conclusion that the resulting financial statements best represent the company's financial condition, results of operations and cash flows
• That the company has complied with all other IFRS standards
• The nature of and the reason for the departure from the standard
• The effects of that departure

4) Related-party disclosures

The IFRS principle of clarity demands that the nature, type, components, and effects of related-party transactions on the company's income and financial position be highlighted in the notes to the financial statements. This includes any outstanding balances owed to and owed from related parties. IAS 24 sets out the extensive required disclosures for related party transactions.

What is a related party?

IAS 24 defines a related party as being "a person, or a member of their family, or company, who directly, or indirectly through another company or person, has some control or significant influence over the company, parent company, subsidiary, associate, joint venture, or fellow subsidiary." In other words, a related party is someone who is related through family ties with or a friend of the major owners or managers of the company or through a related company. In addition, IAS 24 stipulates that a related party can be someone, or a member of their family, or a company, that administers a retirement benefit plan for the company's employees.

What is a related party transaction?

IFRS says that a related party transaction is a "transfer of resources, services or obligations between related parties, regardless of whether a price is charged." This means that even when no price is charged a related party transaction must still be reported between related parties in IFRS financial statements.

Parent-subsidiary relationship disclosures

IFRS requires that relationships between parent companies and their subsidiaries must be disclosed even if there have been no transactions between the related companies. The mere existence of related-party relationships can be important to readers of the financial statements such as vendors, customers, lenders, and employees.

Here IFRS is different from GAAP in requiring disclosures even in the absence of transactions. Examples would include relying on a single customer for a large part of the company's revenue, or dependence on a single supplier for most of its inventory purchases of a unique product.

The company must disclose the name of its parent. If there is a grandparent company, or even a number of companies up the line, then the name of the company that ultimately controls all of them must be disclosed. In addition, if neither the parent nor the ultimate controlling company produces public financial statements, then the name of the next most senior parent company that does produce public financial statements must be disclosed

Other required related-party disclosures include total compensation, short-term employee benefits, post-employment benefits, other long-term benefits, termination benefits, and share-based payments for key management personnel.

Related party transaction disclosures

IFRS requires that the nature of the related party relationship as well as information about the transactions and outstanding balances be disclosed. This will help the reader of the financial statements evaluate the potential effect of the related party relationship on the financial statements by disclosing, at a minimum:

- the amount of the transactions
- the amount of outstanding balances
- any accounts receivable from related parties that may not be collectible
- the terms and conditions including:
    - the description of any collateral
    - the form of payment
    - details of any guarantees given or received

These disclosures must be made separately for the parent company, companies with significant control over the company, subsidiaries, associate companies, joint ventures in which the company is a member, key management personnel of the company or its parent company, and any other related parties.

Subsequent events

The date on the balance sheet is the last day of the accounting period. It usually takes anywhere from a few weeks to a few months to produce the financial statements. Between the closing date and the date the statements are made available, events may occur which must be disclosed when the statements are issued. For example, a notice of bankruptcy may be received a few weeks after year end indicating that a significant customer account has become worthless. This needs to be included in the disclosures of subsequent events.

Contingent liabilities and assets

A contingent liability is a debt which will be owed only if a certain condition is met. For example, if the company has guaranteed a loan for an employee, it will owe the money only if the employee does not repay the loan. In other words, the company's obligation depends on whether the employee pays or not.

Unlike GAAP, IFRS does not allow the recording of these types of contingent liabilities unless the event that can change the contingent liability into a debt has occurred. In other words, IFRS requires that the liability only be recorded when there probably will be a future payment and the amount of the debt can be reliably measured. However, a clear note must disclose relevant information that would have otherwise been presented under GAAP. For example, a loan to the CEO would have to be disclosed in detail because the CEO is a related party and details of the loan would have to be presented, including the likelihood of it being paid.

Other disclosures: IFRS #1

In the first year of adoption of IFRS, if it is not possible for the company to estimate the amount of a required adjustment or its possible effect on future financial statements, then the company must disclose this for every line on the financial statement which has been affected.

The details of dividends proposed or declared must be disclosed. In addition, the details about cumulative preference dividends must also be reported.

Many companies are international in character which is why IFRS requires that details such as the legal name of the company, its domicile and registered address, country of incorporation, the nature of its operations, and the average number of employees during and the total at the end of the accounting period must also be disclosed.

Chapter 6 Summary

- Disclosures required by IFRS provide explanations for investors and are intended to instill confidence in the company.
- The nature of and reason for voluntary changes in accounting policy must disclosed.
- IFRS #1 allows for exceptions in the first year of transition.
- The nature, type, components, and effects of related-party transactions on the company's income and financial position must be highlighted in the notes to the financial statements.
- Events subsequent to the date of the financial statements must be disclosed.
- Contingent liabilities and assets cannot be recorded unless the events on which they depend will probably occur.
- IFRS #1 requires line by line disclosures.

First-time adoption (IFRS #1) 7

IFRS # 1 is the standard that was developed specifically to help companies produce their first IFRS financial statements. It contains many rules that are aimed at making the transition into IFRS a little easier. It also set outs the process for getting there, including details about the first IFRS balance sheet.

1) Opening IFRS balance sheet

The purpose of IFRS #1 is to provide a starting point for IFRS for first-time adopters. The standard requires a financial statement that reconciles the IFRS financial statements to the GAAP financial statements. Publicly accountable enterprises, such as public companies, banks and insurance companies, must comply with IFRS after January 1, 2014 in the US and January 1, 2011 in Canada.

It starts with an opening balance sheet. Under IFRS, the balance sheet is called a "statement of financial position". IFRS #1 says that in its first IFRS statement the company must make an "explicit and unreserved statement of compliance with IFRS." In other words, the company must clearly state that its financial statements were prepared using International Financial Reporting Standards.

IFRS #1 requires that the company have only assets and liabilities on the books that meet all IFRS requirements regardless of GAAP rules. Those items that stay on the balance sheet must be reclassified according to IFRS rules, not GAAP.

Exemptions

The cost/benefit restraint allows companies to be exempt from IFRS rules if the cost outweighs the benefits. Here are some examples:

- avoiding restating items such as business combinations (mergers and acquisitions)
- assets recently restated at fair value under GAAP
- employee benefits
- cumulative currency translation differences
- compound financial instruments (instruments that have both debt and equity elements)
- assets and liabilities of subsidiaries, associates, and joint ventures that exist at the date of transition to IFRS

Business combinations

A business combination is the merger of two or more companies into a single company. In other words, one company "swallows" the other. Often, the company doing the "swallowing" (the purchaser) pays more than the value of the assets. That amount of difference is called "goodwill" and is written off (amortized) over time. Sometimes the company that is being purchased already has "goodwill" in its books. IFRS requires that business combinations must be accounted for using specific rules which include, among others, not changing the classifications that were used under GAAP, and not changing the amount of any goodwill or its amortization period.

Revaluation

IFRS allows companies to use asset values that were restated under GAAP as a result of a specific event, such as privatization or an IPO (initial public offering).

Employee benefits

The company can choose to record the value of any accumulated actuarial gains or losses at the date of transition to IFRS. If this election is made, it must be applied to all employee benefit plans.

Cumulative currency translation differences

This exemption allows companies to not worry about currency differences on the date of transition to IFRS.

Compound financial instruments

Compound financial instruments, such as a convertible bond, normally would be assigned a value for the debt component and another for the conversion feature. Under this exemption, the company is not required to record a liability if the debt is no longer outstanding at the date of transition to IFRS.

Subsidiaries, associates, and joint ventures

If a subsidiary adopts IFRS later than its parent, it must record assets and liabilities at the same amounts as its parent or at the amounts provided under IFRS #1 based on the subsidiary's date of transition to IFRS. If the subsidiary adopts first, the parent must use the same values as the subsidiary.

2) "Current version of IFRS" rule

The first IFRS financial statements must meet all the IFRS that are in place on the effective date of transition to IFRS.

3) Disclosures

In addition to regular IFRS disclosure requirements, the IFRS for first-time adopters requires specific disclosures that explain how the transition from GAAP to IFRS affected the company's reported financial position, financial performance and cash flows.

Disclosures about the transition-period are presented as a separate package that includes a full set of financial statements, financial statement notes that explain the revaluations and reconcile the amounts from GAAP to IFRS, a reconciliation of equity, and profit and loss, from GAAP to IFRS, and a description of the accounting policies applied to the IFRS transition. A first-time adopter must present at least two years of comparative financial data. These requirements as a first-time adopter apply to interim as well as year-end financial statements.

Chapter 7 Summary

• IFRS # 1 is the guideline companies must use to produce their first IFRS financial statements based on the rules that exist on the conversion date.
• The balance sheet is called a "statement of financial position."
• Only assets and liabilities that meet all IFRS requirements regardless of GAAP rules must be on the opening IFRS statement of financial position.
• The cost/benefit restraint allows companies to balance the costs and benefits of the transition to IFRS.
• For business combinations, the classifications that were used under GAAP, and the amount of any goodwill or its amortization period are not changed.
• Disclosures about the transition-period are presented as a separate package that includes reconciliation from GAAP to IFRS.

Exceptions under IFRS #1:

• Companies can use asset values that were restated under GAAP as a result of a specific event.
• The company can choose to record the value of any accumulated actuarial gains or losses at the date of transition to IFRS.
• Companies do not need to worry about currency differences on the date of transition to IFRS.
• For compound financial instruments, the company is not required to record a liability if the debt is no longer outstanding at the date of transition to IFRS.
• A parent company and its subsidiaries, associates, and joint ventures must report the same values for shared assets and liabilities.

IAS and IFRS

8

International Accounting Standards (IAS) and International Financial Reporting Standards (IFRS)

Some standards are called "IFRS" while others are called "IAS". What is the difference? The only difference is that "IAS" were issued from 1973 to 2001 by the International Accounting Standards Committee (IASC) and "IFRS" were issued from 2001 onwards by the International Accounting Standards Board (IASB), the successor of IASC.

The IASB adopted the existing IAS and decided to name any future standards as International Financial Reporting Standards.

The gaps in the IAS numbers are standards that have been withdrawn and replaced with updated ones.

The following pages contain summaries of the accounting standards that are in place at the present time.

Summary of IAS 1: Presentation of Financial Statements

IAS 1 sets out the structure and minimum content of company annual, quarterly and interim financial statements so that investors can compare financial statements covering different accounting periods for the company and have a standard format for comparing financial statements of different companies.

IAS 1 requires that a company present a complete set of financial statements (including the previous year's comparative information) at least once a year.

A complete set of financial statements includes:

(a) a statement of financial position (balance sheet) as at the end of the accounting period
(b) a statement of comprehensive income which includes a statement of results of operations (income statement) for the accounting period
(c) a statement of changes in equity for the accounting period
(d) a statement of cash flows (statement of changes in financial position) for the accounting period
(e) notes outlining significant accounting policies and other explanatory information
(f) a statement of financial position (balance sheet) that goes back to the point before any restatement or reclassification of any items.

IAS 1 stipulates that items presented in the financial statements should be separated into classes of similar items, such as inventory or accounts payable. Items that are not similar must be presented separately, unless they are considered immaterial.

IAS 1 prohibits the offsetting of assets and liabilities, and of income and expenses, unless required or permitted by an IFRS.

IAS 1 requires a company to present all owner changes in equity, such as dividends and issuance of shares, in the statement of changes in equity.

Changes in equity as a result of comprehensive income are required by IAS 1 to be presented in one statement of comprehensive income or in two statements (a separate statement of results of operations and a statement of comprehensive income). The statement of results of operations includes all income and expense items for the period.

IAS 1 requires that the notes to the financial statements must present information about the specific accounting policies used to prepare the financial statements, including how management arrived at estimates and judgments that were used.

IAS 1 requires a company to make an "explicit and unreserved" declaration in the notes that its financial statements comply with all IFRS and have been prepared with the assumption that the company is a "going concern." This means that management does not intend to close and sell the business. Otherwise, management's intention to shut down must be disclosed.

Summary of IAS 2: Inventories

IAS 2 requires that the value of inventory is the lower of cost and "net realizable value". "Net realizable value" is the selling price less completion costs and selling costs. Inventory costs include purchase costs, conversion costs, shipping costs, and other costs to make the inventory available for sale.

IAS 2 requires that the amount of any write-down of inventory costs to net realizable value must be recorded as an expense in the accounting period during which the write-down occurs. If net realizable value goes back up after this write-down, the amount of any reversal of any write-down of inventory must be recorded as a reduction of the expense in the accounting period in which the reversal occurs. This also applies to any inventory losses due to "shrinkage" (theft).

IAS 2 says that the cost of inventory must be assigned by using the "first-in, first-out (FIFO)" or "weighted average" cost formula. "FIFO" assumes that a sold item is the oldest one in inventory and that the cost of that item becomes the cost of goods sold. The "weighted average" formula assigns the average cost of all inventory items at the time of sale to cost of goods sold. The company can designate either costing method to a group of inventory items that are similar and intended for the same use.

IAS 2 requires that the cost of inventory items that are not ordinarily interchangeable must be assigned by using specific identification of their individual costs. This also applies to goods or services produced and segregated for specific projects.

IAS 2 stipulates that, when inventory is sold, the cost of this inventory shall be recorded as an expense in the accounting period in which the related revenue is recorded.

Summary of IAS 7: Statement of Cash Flows

Information about the "cash flows" of the company helps readers of the financial statements assess the timing and certainty of the company's generation of "cash" and "cash equivalents."

IAS 7 defines "cash flows" as the "inflows and outflows of cash and cash equivalents". "Cash" is cash on hand (usually cash in the bank account). "Cash equivalents" are short-term investments that are quickly and easily convertible to known amounts of cash and which are not subject to any significant risk of changes in value (such as currency exchange fluctuation). IAS 7 requires the company to disclose the components of cash and cash equivalents and present a reconciliation of the amounts in its statement of cash flows with the equivalent items reported in the statement of financial position.

IAS 7 stipulates that the cash flow statement separate cash flows into three groups of activities that generate cash or use up cash:

- Operating
- Investing
- Financing activities

Operating activities are the day-to-day revenue-producing activities that are undertaken to provide cash to the company. A company must report cash flows from operating activities using either the direct method where gross cash receipts and gross cash payments are disclosed or the indirect method where the amount of profit or loss is adjusted for the effects of transactions that do not affect cash, such as depreciation and deferred taxes.

The amount of cash flows from operating activities indicates how well the company can pay its bills, keep the doors open, pay dividends and invest in items such as new equipment without having to borrow the money.

Investing activities are the acquisition and disposal of long-term assets and other investments necessary for the company to generate future income. IAS 7 requires that the cash flows arising from obtaining and losing control of other businesses must be presented separately and classified as investing activities.

Financing activities include items that result in changes in form and amount of both shareholder investment in the company and money borrowed by the company. Readers of the financial statements would look at the cash flow from financing activities to see what assets have been pledged as collateral and how vulnerable the company might be to present or future action by creditors.

IAS 7 requires that a company report separately, major classes of gross cash receipts and gross cash payments arising from investing and financing activities.

IAS 7 states that investing and financing transactions that do not require the use of cash or cash equivalents must be excluded from the statement of cash flows. However, they must be disclosed elsewhere in the financial statements.

IAS 7 requires that cash flows resulting from transactions or items held in a foreign currency must be recorded in the company's functional currency (the currency of the country where the company is domiciled) by applying the appropriate exchange rate between the functional currency and the foreign currency at the date the cash flow is generated.

Finally, IAS 7 says that the company must disclose, along with a commentary by management, the amount of significant cash and cash equivalent balances held by the company that are not available for use by the company, such as the minimum cash balance that must be kept on deposit as a condition of a bank loan.

Summary of IAS 8: Accounting Policies, Changes in Accounting Estimates and Errors

Accounting policies are rules the company follows in preparing and presenting financial statements. IAS 8 says that if there is an IFRS standard that is specific to an accounting item, then that standard must be followed. If the item is not specifically covered by an IFRS standard, IAS 8 requires that management use judgment in applying general IFRS principles so that the result will be relevant and reliable information.

IAS 8 requires that the company must apply its accounting policies consistently for similar transactions unless another standard specifically dictates different policies.

IAS 8 does not allow a company to change its accounting policy unless it is required by a specific standard or unless the change produces more reliable and relevant information. If the company chooses to make an accounting change voluntarily, IAS 8 says that it must correct not only the current statement, but also correct any previous statements that are affected by the change to the extent it is practical and affordable to do so.

IFRS recognizes the fact that using reasonable estimates is normal and does not undermine the reliability of the financial statements. A change in accounting estimate adjusts the value of an item reported on the balance sheet because new information is received, such as a change in the amount of oil left in a well.

Prior period errors are material misstatements in and

omissions from the company's financial statements for one or more prior periods that occur as a result of not using reliable information that was available when preparing and presenting the financial statements. Omissions or misstatements of items are material if they could, individually or collectively; influence the decisions of readers of the financial statements. Examples of prior period errors include mathematical mistakes, oversights, and fraud. IAS 8 requires that, as soon as the company discovers the error, the company must correct not only the current statement, but also correct any previous statements that are affected by the change.

Summary of IAS 10: Events after the Reporting Period

IAS 10 defines "events after the reporting period" as those occurring between the close of the accounting period and the date the financial statements are issued. These events (good or bad) can be a confirmation of conditions that existed at the end of the accounting period (called "adjusting" events), such as receiving a bankruptcy notice for a customer the company suspected would not pay. The company should adjust its financial statements to reflect the effect of this confirmation, such as writing off this customer's account receivable to bad debt.

"Events after the reporting period" can be signs of new conditions after the accounting period (called "non-adjusting" events), such as receiving new information that a key supplier of raw material is out of business when you had no hint that this would happen. The company should not adjust its financial statements to reflect the effect of this new information because it really will affect only future items and not the past year's financial statements. However, if this information is material (in other words if it could influence the reader's decisions), then the nature and estimated effect on future financial statements must be disclosed in the notes to the financial statements.

IAS 10 says that a company in trouble should not prepare its financial statements as if it were doing well (in other words, a going concern).

Summary of IAS 11: Construction Contracts

Since most construction contracts are completed over more than one accounting period, the challenge for contractors is deciding when revenue and the costs associated with the contract are recorded in their financial statements.

IAS 11 applies only to construction contracts that relate to the building of a company asset or a group of closely related assets, such as an office building and an adjacent parking lot for employees working in the building. IAS 11 says that each construction contract is accounted for separately. IAS 11 says that in some cases, it might make sense to treat parts of the same contract separately also. For example, the parking lot could be a public one where employees and the public would have to pay for parking.

IAS 11 says that construction contract revenue includes not only the amount of revenue stipulated in the contract, but also any variations such as claims (for example, poor workmanship or faulty materials) and incentive payments (for example, early completion bonus) which must be able to be measured reliably.

IAS 11 says that construction contract costs must be related directly to a specific contract or other costs that are specifically chargeable under the terms of the contract.

The stage of completion of the contract at the end of the reporting period determines how much of the total estimated future revenue and total estimated future expenses are recorded, as long as the estimates are reliable.

If total estimated future revenue and total estimated future expenses cannot be estimated reliably, the amount of revenue that will be recorded will be in the same proportion as the amount of costs that have been incurred to complete the contract. For example, if 40% of the costs to complete the contract have been incurred, then 40% of the revenue is deemed to have been earned and 40% of the total contract revenue is recorded as income in the same period that the costs were incurred.

IAS 11 says that if it is probable that total estimated contract costs will exceed total estimated contract revenue, then the expected loss must be recorded as an expense immediately.

Summary of IAS 12: Income Taxes

IAS 12 defines income taxes as all domestic and foreign taxes payable on the company's taxable profits as well as withholding taxes that are payable by a subsidiary, associate or joint venture. The amount of taxes must be calculated using the tax rates and tax laws in effect at the end of the accounting period.

IAS 12 requires that the current tax due for the current accounting period be recorded as a current liability. However, if installment payments paid during the accounting period exceed the final amount due, then the overpayment is recorded as an asset.

IAS 12 requires that a deferred tax liability be recorded if tax payments are being deferred to a later accounting period. A deferred tax asset must be recorded if tax losses are being carried forward and are expected to be used to reduce taxes in future accounting periods.

IAS 12 says that items not reported in the income statement, such as asset impairments recorded in other comprehensive income and other items recorded directly into equity, are recorded net of taxes.

Summary of IAS 16: Property, Plant and Equipment

IAS 16 says that property, plant, and equipment are tangible assets expected to be used for more that one accounting period which are used in the production or supply of goods or services, or are rented out to customers or other parties, or used internally, such as the company's administrative buildings.

IAS 16 requires that the cost of property, plant, and equipment will be recorded only if future economic benefits, such as contributing to the company's ability to produce cash flow, are probable and can be measured reliably.

The initial cost that is recorded includes the purchase price net of any discounts and rebates, duties, taxes, delivery, and preparation for its intended use. It also includes, as in the case of mining companies, restoring the site to its original condition. However, it does not include financing interest, which is recorded as an expense for the accounting period.

IAS 16 requires that once the purchase of property, plant, and equipment has been recorded, the company must next choose either the "cost model" or the "revaluation model" as the accounting policy that will apply to the entire group of similar property, plant and equipment assets (this group is called a "cash generating unit").

The cost model means that an item of property, plant and equipment is carried at its original cost less any accumulated depreciation and any accumulated impairment losses.

The revaluation model means that an item of property, plant and equipment is carried at its "fair value" (as long as this "fair value" can be measured reliably) less any subsequent accumulated depreciation and subsequent accumulated impairment losses. IAS 16 requires that revaluations must be made at least once a year.

IAS16 says that if an asset's carrying amount is increased or decreased as a result of a revaluation, it is first recorded in the income statement to reverse any previously recorded increases or decreases in value. Any amount left over is then recorded as "other comprehensive income" and accumulated in equity under the heading of "revaluation surplus".

Depreciation is the cost of consuming of an asset over its useful life. IAS 16 requires that this depreciation expense be recorded in the income statement. The method used to calculate the amount of depreciation expense depends on how the asset's future economic benefits are expected to be consumed by the company. For example, if the asset is a piece of manufacturing equipment with an expected useful life of 1,000 hours, and it has run 200 hours this year, then the depreciation expense for the year will be the 20% of the cost (200/1,000).

The residual value of an asset is the amount that the company estimates it will have left over after disposing of the asset, after deducting the estimated costs of disposal. Residual values are usually ignored under IFRS because they are difficult to estimate reliably and are often not material.

IAS 16 requires that an item of property, plant, and equipment no longer be recorded in the balance sheet once that item is sold, or disposed of, or no longer provides future economic benefits.

Summary of IAS 17: Leases

Leases are classified as either a finance lease or an operating lease. A lease is classified as a finance lease if it transfers substantially all the risks and rewards of ownership. A lease is classified as an operating lease if it does not transfer substantially all the risks and rewards of ownership.

IAS 17 says that in the financial statement of the lessee (the company leasing from the lessor and making lease payments) operating lease payments should be recorded as an expense. For a finance lease, the lessee will record the item leased as an asset based on the lower of its fair value or the present value of the total of the lease payments, using the interest rate implicit in the lease, along with a corresponding liability for the total of the lease payments. The lease payments reduce the liability and depreciation expense that is recorded for the leased asset. IAS 17 requires that if there is no reasonable certainty that the lessee will obtain ownership by the end of the lease term, the asset must be fully depreciated (expensed) over the shorter of the lease term and its useful life.

IAS 17 says that in the financial statement of the lessor (the company leasing to the lessee and receiving the lease payments) a depreciation expense is recorded for an operating lease asset and the lease payments are recorded as income. For a finance lease, a receivable is recorded for the balance of the lease payments.

Summary of IAS 18: Revenue

IAS 18 requires that revenue be recorded when it is probable that future economic benefits will flow to the company and these benefits can be measured reliably. Revenue is the product of the sale of goods, the rendering of services, and the use by others of company assets resulting in interest, royalties and dividends.

IAS 18 says that revenue must be measured at the fair value of the consideration received or receivable. Fair value is the amount for which an asset could be exchanged, or a liability settled, based on the agreement between knowledgeable, willing parties in an arm's length transaction.

IAS 18 stipulates that revenue from the sale of goods be recorded only when all of the following conditions have been met:

1. The company has transferred to the buyer the significant risks and rewards of ownership of the goods
2. The company does not retain any effective control over the goods sold
3. The amount of revenue can be measured reliably
4. The company will probably collect its money
5. The costs related to the transaction can be measured reliably.

IAS 18 stipulates that revenue from the rendering of services be recorded only when all of the following conditions have been met:

1. The amount of revenue can be measured reliably

2. The company will probably collect its money

3. The stage of completion of the contract at the end of the reporting period can be measured reliably

4. The costs related to the transaction and the costs to complete the contract can be measured reliably.

Recording revenue based on the stage of completion of a contract is called the "percentage of completion" method. Under this method, revenue is recorded in the accounting periods in which the services are rendered. IAS 18 requires that when the total revenue and expenses related to a contract involving the rendering of services cannot be estimated reliably, only the amount of billings to the customer is recorded as revenue.

IAS 18 requires that interest revenue must be recorded using the effective interest method as set out in IAS 39. IAS 18 requires that royalty revenue must be recorded as due according to the royalty agreement. IAS 18 requires that dividend revenue must be recorded when the shareholder's right to receive payment is established (when the dividend is declared).

Summary of IAS 19: Employee Benefits

IAS 19 defines employee benefits as all forms of consideration given by a company in exchange for service rendered by employees. IAS 19 requires that a company must record a liability when an employee has provided service in exchange for employee benefits to be paid in the future and an expense when the company consumes the economic benefit arising from the service provided by an employee in exchange for employee benefits.

IAS 19 defines post-employment benefits as employee benefits (other than termination benefits) which are payable after the completion of employment. Post-employment benefit plans can be either formal or informal. Post-employment benefit plans are classified as either defined contribution plans or defined benefit plans.

Under a defined contribution plan, the company pays fixed contributions to a separate pension plan administrator or fund. The company has no obligation to pay any further contributions if the fund does not hold sufficient assets to pay all the employee benefits. IAS 19 requires that the company record a contribution payable based on the services rendered by the employee.

Under a defined benefit plan, the company's obligation is to provide the agreed benefits to current and former employees. The company's obligation is increased to meet any shortfall in funding benefits. Using actuarial techniques to make a reliable estimate of the present value of the amount of benefit that employees have earned in return for their service in the current and prior accounting periods, the company establishes the fair value of the plan assets. Any increase or decrease in the value of the plan assets is recorded as a gain or loss. If a company has more than one defined benefit plan, these procedures are applied to each plan separately.

IAS 19 defines "other long-term employee benefits" as employee benefits (other than post-employment benefits and termination benefits) which do not fall due in full within twelve months after the end of the accounting period in which the employee renders the related service.

IAS 19 defines termination benefits as employee benefits payable as a result of either the termination of an employee's employment before the normal retirement date, or an employee's decision to accept early retirement in exchange for those benefits. IAS 19 requires that the company record the termination benefits as a liability and an expense when, and only when, there is evidence that the company will terminate the employment of an employee or group of employees before the normal retirement date, or will provide termination benefits as a result of an offer made in order to encourage early retirement.

Summary of IAS 20: Accounting for Government Grants and Disclosure of Government Assistance

IAS 20 defines government grants as government assistance in the form of transfers of resources (usually money) to a company in return for meeting the assistance program criteria established by the government. The government grant may be in the form of the transfer of a non-monetary asset, such as land. In that case, the grant and the asset are assessed at the non-monetary asset's fair value.

IAS 20 says you should not include government assistance which cannot be measured reliably, normal transactions with the government, or the provision of infrastructure such as roads or bridges.

IAS 20 requires that the company record the government grant as revenue. If the government grant is conditional on being used to purchase an asset, then the asset purchased with the grant is recorded at its fair value less the amount of the grant to reflect the real cost of the asset, or the asset is recorded at its full cost and the grant is recorded as deferred income. Any grants still to be received after the purchase of the assets are recorded as a receivable. If the government grant is conditional on producing a particular type or level of income, then the grant is recorded as additional income if the conditions are met.

IAS 20 and IAS 8 require that a government grant that becomes repayable must be accounted for as a revision to an accounting estimate by first removing any existing related government grant credit already on the balance sheet, and any additional repayment amount is recorded as an expense.

Repayment of a grant related to an asset must be recorded by increasing the carrying amount of the asset or reducing the deferred income balance by the amount repayable.

IAS 20 requires the following disclosures related to government grants:

1. The accounting policy adopted for government grants, including the methods of presentation adopted in the financial statements.
2. The nature and extent of government grants recorded in the financial statements and a description of the forms of government assistance received by the company.
3. Unfulfilled conditions of government assistance that have been recorded.

Summary of IAS 21:
The Effects of Changes in Foreign Exchange Rates

A company may carry on foreign activities by having transactions in foreign currencies, by having foreign operations, or by presenting its financial statements in a foreign currency. IAS 21 defines a "foreign operation" as a company that is a subsidiary, associate, joint venture or branch operating in a different country or currency.

IAS 21 does not apply to hedge accounting for foreign currency items, which is covered by IAS 39, nor does it apply to the presentation of the foreign currency cash flows in the cash flow statement, which is covered by IAS 7.

IAS 21 says that "functional currency" is the currency in which the company primarily generates and spends cash. In other words, functional currency is the currency in which sales prices for its goods and services are denominated and collected, and the currency in which it pays for materials, labor and other expenses. "Foreign currency" is a currency other than the functional currency of the company. The "exchange difference" is the difference between the "functional currency" and a "foreign currency." IAS 21 requires that exchange differences be recorded in the income statement.

IAS 21 requires that the company report at the end of each accounting period all foreign currency monetary items using the closing exchange rate on the last day of the accounting period, all non-monetary items that are measured using historical cost in a foreign currency must be reported using the exchange rate on the date of the transaction, and all non-monetary items that are measured at fair value in a foreign currency must be recorded using the exchange rates on the date when the fair value was determined.

IAS 21 defines "net investment in a foreign operation" as the amount of the company's interest in the net assets of a foreign operation. A foreign currency transaction must be recorded with the initial investment using the market exchange rate on the date of the transaction. Exchange differences related to the net investment in a foreign operation may be recorded either in the company's income statement or the individual financial statements of the foreign operation. In consolidated financial statements which include a foreign subsidiary, exchange differences must be recorded in other comprehensive income. When the company disposes of its net investment in a foreign operation, it must record a profit or loss on the disposal.

IAS 21 permits the company to present its financial statements in any currency (or currencies) it wants to. If the presentation currency differs from the company's functional currency, it must record its income statement and balance sheet in the presentation currency. A common currency must be used when income statements and balance sheets of individual companies with different functional currencies are rolled up into consolidated financial statements.

IAS 21 requires that if the functional currency is the currency of a hyperinflationary economy, the company's financial statements must be restated in accordance with IAS 29 "Financial Reporting in Hyperinflationary Economies."

Summary of IAS 23: Borrowing Costs

Borrowing costs are interest and other costs incurred when borrowing funds.

IAS 23 says that borrowing costs that are directly attributable to the acquisition, construction or production of a "qualifying asset" become part of the capitalized cost of that asset. A "qualifying asset" is an asset that takes a substantial period of time to get ready for its intended use or sale, such as a newly purchased existing manufacturing plant that must be modified before it can be used. Other borrowing costs are recorded as an expense.

IAS 23 says that borrowing costs for qualifying assets can only be capitalized if all of the following conditions are met:

1. The company incurs expenditures for the asset
2. The company incurs borrowing costs
3. The company prepares the asset for its intended use or sale

IAS 21 requires that the company must suspend capitalizing borrowing costs when it suspends active development of a qualifying asset. IAS 21 requires that the company stop capitalizing borrowing costs when all the activities necessary to prepare the qualifying asset for its intended use or sale are substantially complete.

IAS 21 requires that the company disclose the amount of borrowing costs capitalized during the accounting period and the method for determining which borrowing costs were eligible for capitalization.

Summary of IAS 24: Related Party Disclosures

IAS 24 requires that a company's financial statements must contain the disclosures necessary to draw attention to the possibility that its financial position and profit or loss may have been affected by the existence of related parties and by transactions and outstanding balances with such parties.

IAS 24 says that a party is related to the company if one of the following applies:

1. The party directly or indirectly, through one or more intermediaries it controls,

    a. is controlled by the company (this includes parents, subsidiaries and fellow subsidiaries)

    or

    b. has an interest in the company that gives it significant influence over the company

    or

    c. has joint control over the company

2. The party is an associate of the company (as defined in IAS 28 Investments in Associates).

3. The party is a joint venture in which the company is a participant (IAS 31 Interests in Joint Ventures).

4. The party is a member of the key management

personnel of the company or its parent.

5. The party is a close friend or member of the family of any individual having control.

6. The party is a post-employment benefit plan for the benefit of employees of the company

IAS 24 defines a related party transaction as a transfer of resources, services or obligations between related parties, regardless of whether a price is charged. It also defines "close members of the family" as those family members who may be expected to influence, or be influenced by, an individual in their dealings with the company, which may include the individual's domestic partner and children, children of the individual's domestic partner, and dependants of the individual or the individual's domestic partner.

IAS 24 requires that relationships between parent companies and subsidiaries must be disclosed irrespective whether or not there have been transactions between those related parties.

A company must disclose the name of the company's parent and, if different, the ultimate controlling party. If neither the company's parent nor the ultimate controlling party produces financial statements available for public use, the name of the next most senior parent company that does so must also be disclosed.

IAS 24 requires that a company must disclose key management personnel compensation in total and for each of the following categories:

1. Short-term employee benefits
2. Post-employment benefits
3. Other long-term benefits
4. Termination benefits
5. Share-based payments

In addition to the requirements to disclose key management personnel compensation, under IAS 24, the company must disclose if there have been transactions between related parties, the nature of the related party relationship as well as information about the transactions and any outstanding balances. These disclosures are intended to explain the potential effect of the relationship on the financial statements. These disclosure requirements are at a minimum:

1. The amount of the transactions

2. The amount of outstanding balances
  a. Their terms and conditions, including whether they are secured, and the nature of the consideration to be provided in settlement
  b. Details of any guarantees given or received

3. Provisions for doubtful debts related to the amount of outstanding balances

4. The expense recorded during the accounting period for doubtful debts due from related parties

IAS 24 stipulates that these disclosures must be made separately for the parent, companies with joint control or significant influence over the company, subsidiaries, associates, joint ventures in which the company is a participant, key management personnel of the company or its parent, and other related parties.

Summary of IAS 26:
Accounting and Reporting by Retirement Benefit Plans

IAS 26 applies to the financial statements of retirement benefit plans. The financial statements must explain the relationship between the actuarial present value of promised retirement benefits and the net assets available for benefits, and the policy for the funding of promised benefits.

IAS 26 requires that the financial statements of a retirement benefit plan, whether defined benefit or defined contribution, must contain a statement of changes in net assets available for benefits, a summary of significant accounting policies, and a description of the plan and the effect of any changes in the plan during the period.

IAS 26 defines retirement benefit plans as arrangements to provide benefits for employees on or after termination of service, either in the form of an annual income or as a lump sum.

IAS 26 requires that the financial statements of a defined contribution plan must contain a statement of net assets available for benefits and a description of the funding policy.

IAS 26 requires that the financial statements of a defined benefit plan must contain either:

    1. a statement that shows:
        a. the net assets available for benefits
        b. the actuarial present value of promised retirement benefits, distinguishing between

vested benefits and non-vested benefits and
c. the resulting excess or deficit

or

2. a statement of net assets available for benefits including either:

a. a note disclosing the actuarial present value of promised retirement benefits, distinguishing between vested benefits and non-vested benefits

or

b. a reference to this information in an accompanying actuarial report

If an actuarial valuation has not been prepared at the date of the financial statements, the most recent valuation must be used as a base and the date of the valuation disclosed.

The actuarial present value of promised retirement benefits must be based on the benefits promised under the terms of the plan and service rendered to date using either current salary levels or projected salary levels with a disclosure of the basis used. IAS 26 requires that the effect of any changes in actuarial assumptions that has a significant effect on the actuarial present value of promised retirement benefits must also be disclosed.

IAS 26 requires that retirement benefit plan investments be carried at fair value. In the case of marketable securities fair value is market value. Where plan investments are held for which an estimate of fair value is not possible, IAS 26 requires that the company disclose why fair value is not used.

Summary of IAS 27:
Consolidated and Separate Financial Statements

IAS 27 defines "consolidated financial statements" as the financial statements of a group of companies presented as a single company. A group consists of a parent company and all its subsidiaries. A subsidiary is a company, including an unincorporated company such as a partnership that is controlled by another company (known as the parent). Control is the power to set the financial and operating policies of a company.

IAS 27 requires that a parent company must consolidate its investments in subsidiaries and present the financial statements as if all the companies were a single company, line item by line item, using uniform accounting policies for reporting similar transactions and events. Inter-company transactions and balances between companies within the group must be eliminated.

IAS 27 requires that non-controlling interests must be presented in the consolidated balance sheet within equity, separately from the equity of the owners of the parent. Total comprehensive income must be allocated to the owners of the parent and to the non-controlling interests.

IAS 27 specifies that changes in a parent's ownership interest in a subsidiary that do not result in the loss of control are recorded as changes in equity. IAS 27 requires that when a parent loses control of a subsidiary, it must remove from its financial statements the assets and liabilities and related equity items of the former subsidiary. Any gain or loss is recorded in the income statement. Any investment retained in the former subsidiary is measured at its fair value at the date when control is lost.

IAS 27 requires that investments in subsidiaries, jointly controlled entities and associates must be accounted for at cost or in accordance with IAS 39 (Financial Instruments: Recognition and Measurement).

IAS 27 requires that a company must disclose information about the nature of the relationship between the parent company and its subsidiaries.

Summary of IAS 28: Investments in Associates

"Associates" are companies related through ownership investment. IAS 28 explains how to account for investments in associates but it does not apply to investments in associates held by venture capital organizations, or mutual funds, unit trusts and similar firms.

IAS 28 requires that investments in associates be recorded at fair value in accordance with IAS 39 (Financial Instruments: Recognition and Measurement), with changes in fair value recorded in the income statement in the accounting period in which the change occurred.

IAS 28 defines "significant influence" as "the power to participate in the financial and operating policy decisions of the investee, but it is not control or joint control over those policies." In other words, the company has some say in how the company runs, but the final decision rests with the associate company.

IAS 28 says that an investor company holding, directly or indirectly through subsidiaries, 20 per cent or more of the voting power of an investee company is presumed to have significant influence over the investee company. A substantial or majority ownership by another investor company does not necessarily prevent an investor company from having significant influence.

IAS 28 specifies that the equity method must be used to record the investment in an associate at cost. After the date of acquisition, the carrying amount of the investment is increased or decreased to record the investor company's share of the profit or loss of the investee company. The investor company's share of the profit or loss of the investee company is recorded in the investor company's profit or loss.

IAS 28 says that when dividends are received from an investee company, the carrying amount of the investment is reduced accordingly. Adjustments to the carrying amount of the investment must be made to reflect changes in the investee company's other comprehensive income which are a result of the revaluation of property, plant and equipment and from foreign exchange differences. The investor company's share of those changes is recorded in its own "other comprehensive income" (IAS 1: Presentation of Financial Statements).

IAS 28 requires that the investor company's financial statements must reflect any impairment loss of the investor company's net investment in the associate.

IAS 28 specifies that when separate financial statements are prepared, investments in subsidiaries, jointly controlled entities and associates that are not classified as "held for sale" must be recorded, for each category of investments, either at cost, or in accordance with IAS 39 (Financial Instruments Recognition and Measurement).

IAS 28 requires that investments in subsidiaries, jointly controlled entities and associates that are classified as "held for sale" must be recorded using IFRS 5 (Non-current Assets Held for Sale and Discontinued Operations).IAS 28 stipulates that investments in jointly controlled entities and associates that are accounted for using IAS 39 in the consolidated financial statements must be accounted for in the same way in the investor company's separate financial statements.

Summary of IAS 29:
Financial Reporting in Hyperinflationary Economies

IAS 29 applies to the financial statements, including the consolidated financial statements, of any company whose functional currency is the currency of a hyperinflationary economy. IAS 29 does not provide the rate that is deemed to be inflationary, but leaves it up to the company to judge whether the economy is hyperinflationary and whether a restatement of financial statements is required.

IAS 29 suggests that some of the characteristics of a hyperinflationary economy are:

1. the general population prefers to keep its wealth in non-monetary assets or in a relatively stable foreign currency

2. the general population regards monetary amounts not in terms of the local currency but in terms of a relatively stable foreign currency and prices may be quoted in that currency

3. sales and purchases on credit take place at prices that compensate for the expected loss of purchasing power during the credit repayment period, even if the period is short

4. interest rates, wages and prices are linked to a price index

5. the cumulative inflation rate over three years is approaching, or exceeds, 100%

IAS 29 requires that the financial statements of a company whose functional currency is the currency of a hyperinflationary economy must be stated in the value of the currency that was in effect at the end of the accounting period, not the value of the currency when the financial statements are issued, for both the current and previous period comparative amounts. This must be clearly disclosed in the financial statements.

IAS 29 requires that a company use a general price index that reflects changes in general purchasing power when restating its financial statements. IAS 29 recommends that that all companies that produce their financial statements in the currency of the same economy use the same index.

When an economy ceases to be hyperinflationary and the company discontinues the preparation and presentation of financial statements based on IAS 29, it must use the same currency unit that it used at the end of the current accounting period as the basis for the carrying amounts in its subsequent financial statements.

Summary of IAS 31: Interests in Joint Ventures

IAS 31 applies to "joint ventures." A "joint venture" is a contractual arrangement among two or more companies to operate under joint control. "Joint control" exists only when the strategic financial and operating decisions require the unanimous consent of the companies sharing control (the "venturers"). However, IAS 31 does not apply to venture capital firms, mutual funds, unit trusts and similar firms.

IAS 31 requires that investments in joint ventures be recorded at fair value in accordance with IAS 39 (Financial Instruments: Recognition and Measurement), with changes in fair value recorded in the income statement in the accounting period in which the change occurred.

"Jointly controlled operations" are joint ventures that are an arrangement to pool assets and other resources rather than forming a separate firm, with all the "venturers" using their own assets, incurring their own expenses and liabilities and raising their own finance. IAS 31 requires that each "venturer" record in its own financial statements the assets that it controls and the liabilities that it incurs as well as the expenses that it incurs and its share of the income that it earns from the sale of goods or services by the joint venture.

Some joint ventures involve the joint control, and often the joint ownership, by the venturers of one or more assets of the joint venture. Each venturer may take its share of profit and each is responsible for its share of the expenses. IAS 31 requires that each "venturer" record in its own financial statements its share of the jointly controlled assets, any liabilities that it has incurred, its share of any liabilities incurred jointly with the other venturers, and its share of sales or income and expenses.

A "jointly controlled" venture is a corporation, partnership or other firm owned by "venturers." IAS 31 requires that each "venturer" must record its interest in a jointly controlled venture using either the "proportionate consolidation" method or the "equity" method.

"Proportionate consolidation" means that each "venturer's" share of liabilities, income and expenses of a jointly controlled venture is combined line by line with similar items in the "venturer's" financial statements or reported as separate line items in the "venturer's" financial statements.

The equity method means that the investment in a jointly controlled venture is initially recorded at cost and adjusted for any subsequent changes in the net worth of the of the jointly controlled venture. The "venturer's" share of the jointly controlled venture's profit or loss is included in the "venturer's" income statement.

IAS 31 requires that the "venturer" must record the full amount of any loss for any contribution or sale of assets when there is evidence of a reduction in the "net realizable value" (market value) of current assets or when there is evidence an impairment loss (drop in fair value).

IAS 31 specifies that when a "venturer" purchases assets from a joint venture, the "venturer" must not record its share of the profits of the joint venture from the transaction until it resells the assets to an independent party.

IAS 31 says that a "venturer" must record its share of the losses resulting from these transactions in the same way as profits except that losses must be recorded immediately when they represent a reduction in the "net realizable value" (market value) of current assets or an impairment loss (drop in fair value).

IAS 31 requires that when separate financial statements are prepared, investments in subsidiaries, jointly controlled ventures and associates that are not classified as "held for sale" must be recorded either at cost or using IAS 39 (Financial Instruments Recognition and Measurement) for each category of investments while those that classified as "held for sale" must be accounted for in accordance with IFRS 5 (Non-current Assets Held for Sale and Discontinued Operations).

IAS 31 stipulates that investments in jointly controlled ventures and associates that are accounted for using IAS 39 (Financial Instruments Recognition and Measurement) in the consolidated financial statements must be accounted for in the same way in the investor's separate financial statements.

Summary of IAS 32: Financial Instruments Presentation

IAS 32 requires that the issuer of a financial instrument must classify the instrument, or its component parts, on initial recording as a financial liability, a financial asset or an equity instrument in accordance with the substance of the contractual arrangement. An equity instrument is any contract that provides some ownership in a company.

IAS 32 specifies that the issuer of a non-derivative financial instrument must evaluate the terms of the financial instrument to determine whether it contains both a liability and an equity component. These components must be classified separately as financial liabilities, financial assets or equity instruments.

IAS 32 says that a financial instrument is any contract that is recorded as a financial asset of one company and a financial liability or equity instrument of another company.

According to IAS 32, a financial asset can be:

1. cash

2. an equity instrument (usually a share) of another company

3. a contractual right:

> a. to receive cash or another financial asset from another company
>
> b. to exchange financial assets or financial

liabilities with another company under potentially favorable conditions

c. a contract that may be settled in the company's own equity instruments and is:

    i. a non-derivative for which the company may be obliged to receive a number of the company's own equity instruments

    OR

    ii. a derivative that may be settled other than by the exchange of a fixed amount of cash or another financial asset for the company's own equity instruments

IAS 32 says that a financial liability is any liability that is:

1. a contractual obligation:

    a. to deliver cash or another financial asset to another company

    OR

    b. to exchange financial assets or financial liabilities with another company under potentially unfavorable conditions

2. a contract that may be settled in the company's own equity instruments and is:

a. a non-derivative for which the company may be obliged to deliver a number of the company's own equity instruments.

OR

b. a derivative that may be settled other than by the exchange of cash or another financial asset for a fixed number of the company's own equity instruments.

IAS 32 says that when a derivative financial instrument gives one party a choice over how it is settled (the issuer or the holder can choose settlement in cash or by exchanging shares for cash), it is a financial asset, a financial liability, or an equity instrument.

IAS 32 requires that any shares ("treasury shares") a company reacquires must be deducted from equity. No gain or loss is recorded on the purchase, sale, issue or cancellation of a company's own shares. Payment received for treasury shares must be recorded directly in equity.

IAS 32 specifies that interest, dividends, losses and gains relating to a financial instrument or a component that is a financial liability must be recorded as income or expense in the income statement.

IAS 32 requires that any dividends to shareholders must be recorded as a deduction from equity, net of any income tax benefit and transaction costs.

Financial instruments can be netted out only under limited conditions. IAS 32 stipulates that a financial asset and a financial liability must be offset and the net amount presented in the balance sheet only when a company:

1. currently has a legally enforceable right to set off the recorded amounts.

AND

2. intends either to settle on a net basis, or to keep the asset and settle the liability simultaneously.

Summary of IAS 33: Earnings per Share

IAS 33 applies to companies whose "ordinary shares" and "potential ordinary shares" are publicly traded and therefore must calculate and disclose earnings per share. An "ordinary share" is a share that is usually referred to as a "common share." A "potential ordinary share" is a financial instrument or other contract that may entitle its holder to ordinary shares, such as a convertible bond.

IAS 33 requires that a company must present in its statement of comprehensive income both "basic" and "diluted" earnings per share for each class of shareholders for all accounting periods presented. IAS 33 stipulates that a company reporting a discontinued operation must disclose the basic and diluted amounts per share for the discontinued operation either in the statement of comprehensive income or in the notes.

IAS 33 requires that "basic" earnings per share must be calculated by dividing after-tax profit or loss (the numerator) by the weighted average number of ordinary shares outstanding (the denominator) during the accounting period.

IAS 33 requires that "diluted" earnings per share must be calculated by adjusting profit or loss for the effects of all "dilutive" potential ordinary shares. Dilution is a reduction in earnings per share or an increase in loss per share resulting from the assumption that convertible instruments are converted, that options or warrants are exercised.

IAS 33 states that potential ordinary shares must be treated as dilutive when, and only when, their conversion to ordinary shares would decrease earnings per share or increase loss per share from continuing operations.

IAS 33 requires that if the number of ordinary or potential ordinary shares outstanding increases as a result of a capitalization (additional shareholder investment), bonus issue or share split, or decreases as a result of a reverse share split, the calculation of basic and diluted earnings per share for all accounting periods presented must be adjusted retrospectively (restating previous periods).

Summary of IAS 34: Interim Financial Reporting

IAS 34 applies to companies that publish an IFRS "interim financial report." "Interim financial report" means a financial report containing either a complete set of financial statements (that comply with IFRS #1), or a set of "condensed" financial statements. "Condensed" financial statements contain information on new activities, events, and circumstances. An "interim" period is shorter than a full financial year.

IAS 34 requires that an interim financial report must include:

(a) a "condensed" statement of financial position
(b) a "condensed" statement of comprehensive income that includes:
    (i) a "condensed" single statement
    or
    (ii) a "condensed" statement of results of operations and a "condensed" statement of comprehensive income
(c) a "condensed" statement of changes in equity
(d) a "condensed" statement of cash flows
(e) selected explanatory notes.

IAS 34 stipulates that a set of "condensed" financial statements published in its interim financial report must include each of the headings, subtotals and selected explanatory notes that were included in its most recent annual financial statements.

IAS 34 says that materiality, reliability, and relevance will be the deciding factors in whether and how an item will disclosed, measured, and classified. There may be a greater need to rely on estimates in interim financial reports.

In addition, IAS 34 requires that a company apply the same accounting policies in its interim financial statements as are applied in its annual financial statements.

Summary of IAS 36: Impairment of Assets

"Impairment" means a material change (either up or down) in value. IAS 36 requires that a company must assess at the end of each accounting period whether there is any sign that an asset may be "impaired" and, if yes, estimate the change in value of that asset.

This impairment test may be performed at any time during an annual period, provided it is performed at the same time every year. If it is not possible to estimate the change of an individual asset, a company must instead estimate the change in value of the "cash-generating unit" to which the asset belongs. A "cash-generating unit" is the group of similar assets.

For intangible assets, IAS 36 demands that even when there is no hint of impairment, a company must test annually an intangible asset with an indefinite useful life, or an intangible asset not yet available for use, for impairment by comparing its book value (carrying amount) with its recoverable amount (fair value). The recoverable amount of an asset or a cash-generating unit is the higher of its "fair value less costs to sell" and its "value in use."

"Fair value less costs to sell" is the amount for which an asset or cash-generating unit could be sold in an arm's length transaction between knowledgeable, willing parties, less the costs of disposal.

"Value in use" is the present value and timing of the future cash flows expected to be produced by an asset or cash-generating unit. It is calculated by estimating. Different intangible assets may be tested for impairment at different times. IAS 36 specifically mentions that goodwill acquired in a business combination must be tested for impairment annually.

IAS 36 says that estimates of future cash flows for the asset in its current condition must include projections of cash inflows from the use of the asset and net cash flows, if any, to be received for the disposal of the asset at the end of its useful life, but not improving or enhancing the asset's performance.

IAS 36 stipulates that if, and only if, the recoverable amount of an asset is less than its carrying amount (book value), the carrying amount of the asset must be reduced to its recoverable amount. That reduction is recorded as an impairment loss. The impairment loss must be recorded immediately in the income statement. For a cash-generating unit, the impairment loss must be recorded to reduce the carrying amount of the assets of the unit in the following order: first, to reduce the carrying amount of any goodwill allocated to the cash-generating unit and then to the other assets of the unit.

IAS 36 requires that a company not reduce the carrying amount of an asset below the highest of:

a) its fair value less costs to sell
b) its value in use
c) zero.

IAS 36 says that goodwill acquired in a business acquisition must be allocated to each of the acquirer's cash-generating units that are expected to benefit from the combination.

IAS 36 stipulates that a company must assess at the end of each accounting reporting period whether there is any indication that an impairment loss recorded in a previous accounting period has reversed itself. If yes, it must record that reversal immediately in the income statement. The only exception is an impairment loss recorded for goodwill which cannot be reversed in a subsequent period.

Summary of IAS 37:
Provisions, Contingent Liabilities and Contingent Assets

A provision is a liability of which the timing or the exact amount is uncertain.

IAS 37 requires that a provision must be recorded when, and only when, a company has a present obligation as a result of a past event, or it is probable (more likely than not) that obligation will have to be paid, or a reliable estimate can be made of the amount of the obligation. After the most likely outcome has been determined, a provision equal to the amount to settle the obligation at the end of the reporting period must be recorded.

IAS 37 stipulates that a "contingent liability" is a possible obligation which will be confirmed only by uncertain future events. A "contingent liability" can also be a present obligation not recorded either because it is not probable that a payment will be required to settle the obligation or because the amount of the obligation cannot be measured reliably. IAS 37 further stipulates that a company must not record a contingent liability, but must disclose a contingent liability.

A "contingent asset" is a possible asset whose existence will be confirmed only by future events. IAS 37 says that a company must not record a contingent asset.

Summary of IAS 38: Intangible Assets

An "intangible asset" is an "identifiable asset" without physical substance. An asset is "identifiable" if it is "separable" (capable of being separated from the company and sold, transferred, licensed, rented or exchanged).

IAS 38 requires that an intangible asset must be recorded if, and only if it is probable that the asset will produce expected future economic benefits for the company and the cost of the asset can be measured reliably.

IAS 38 stipulates that an intangible asset must be measured initially at cost which includes its purchase price, import duties, non-refundable purchase taxes, after deducting trade discounts and rebates and any associated cost of preparing the asset for its intended use.

IAS 38 says that any intangible asset produced as a result of research must not be recorded as an asset. Research must be recorded as an expense when it is incurred. On the other hand, IAS 38 requires that an intangible asset produced as a result of development must be recorded if, and only if, it is technically feasible and resources are available to complete the intangible asset so that it will be available for use or sale, that the company intends to complete the intangible asset and can use or sell it, and the amount of probable future economic benefits can be measured reliably. In other words, there must be a market for the output of the intangible asset (or the intangible asset itself) or, if it is to be used internally, the usefulness of the intangible asset must be able to be measured reliably.

IAS 38 stipulates that internally generated brands, mastheads, publishing titles, customer lists and similar items must not be recorded as intangible assets.

IAS 38 requires that a company must choose either the cost model or the revaluation model as its accounting policy for intangible assets. If an intangible asset is accounted for using the revaluation model, then all the other assets in its class must also be accounted for using the same model, unless there is no "active market" for those assets. An "active market" is a market in which the items traded in the market are all the same, where willing buyers and sellers can normally be found at any time, and prices are available to the public.

If using the cost model, IAS 38 requires that, after initial recognition, an intangible asset must be carried at its cost less any accumulated amortization and any accumulated impairment losses. If using the revaluation model, IAS 38 requires that, after initial recognition, an intangible asset must be carried at a revalued amount, being its fair value at the date of the revaluation less any subsequent accumulated amortization and any subsequent accumulated impairment losses.

IAS 38 says that if an intangible asset's carrying amount is increased as a result of a revaluation, the increase must be recorded in "other comprehensive income" and accumulated in equity under the heading of "revaluation surplus." However, if it reverses a revaluation decrease of the same asset previously recorded in the income statement, then the increase must also be recorded in the income statement.

IAS 38 says that if an intangible asset's carrying amount

is decreased as a result of a revaluation, the decrease must be recorded in the income statement. However, the decrease must be recorded in "other comprehensive income" to the extent of any credit balance in the "revaluation surplus" related to that asset.

The "useful life" is the period over which an asset is expected to be available for use by a company or the number of production units expected to be obtained from the asset by the company. Useful life can either be "finite" (limited) or "indefinite" (unlimited).

IAS 38 requires a company to assess whether the "useful life" of an intangible asset is finite or indefinite and, if finite, the length of that "useful life", or the potential number of production units expected during that "useful life." An intangible asset will be deemed to have an indefinite "useful life" when the asset is expected to generate net cash inflows indefinitely for the company.

IAS 38 requires that the "depreciable amount" (the cost of an asset less its "residual value") of an intangible asset with a finite useful life must be expensed systematically over its useful life. (This expense is called "depreciation" for tangible assets and "amortization" for intangible assets). Amortization must begin when the asset is available for use and end when either the asset is classified as held for sale or the asset is written off, whichever comes first.

The residual value of an intangible asset is the estimated amount that the company would currently obtain from disposal of the asset, after deducting the estimated costs of disposal, if the asset were already at the end of its useful life.

IAS 38 requires that the residual value of an intangible asset with a finite useful life must be assumed to be zero unless there is a commitment by a third party to purchase the asset at the end of its useful life or there is value in an active market.

IAS 38 requires that that unless a more reliable way can be found, the "straight-line method" (evenly over its useful life) must be used. The amortization expense must be recorded in the income statement. The amortization must be revaluated and adjusted if it has changed.

IAS 38 requires that an intangible asset with an indefinite useful life must not be recorded. However, IAS 36 "Impairment of Assets" requires a company to test an existing intangible asset with an indefinite useful life for impairment by comparing its recoverable amount with its carrying amount annually and whenever there is an indication that the intangible asset may be impaired.

IAS 38 stipulates that the useful life of an intangible asset that is not being amortized must be reviewed each accounting period.

Summary of IAS 39:
Financial Instruments Recognition and Measurement

IAS 39 requires that a company record a financial asset or a financial liability in its statement of financial position when, and only when, the company incurs a contractual obligation (liability) or receives a contractual right (asset) based on the terms of the financial instrument.

IAS 39 requires that a company remove a financial liability from its statement of financial position when, and only when the obligation specified in the contract is paid, cancelled, or expires.

IAS 39 stipulates that when a financial asset or financial liability is recorded initially, a company must measure it at its "fair value" plus related transaction costs. "Fair value" is the amount for which an asset could be exchanged, or a liability settled, between knowledgeable, willing parties in an arm's length transaction.

IAS 39 specifies that after initial recognition, a company must measure financial assets, at their fair values, without any deduction for transaction costs it may incur on sale or other disposal, except for loans and receivables, held-to-maturity investments (measured at amortized cost using the effective interest method), investments in equity instruments that do not have a quoted market price in an active market and whose fair value cannot be reliably measured, and derivatives (measured at cost).

IAS 39 specifies that, after initial recognition, a company must in most cases measure financial liabilities at amortized cost using the effective interest method.

IAS 39 requires that a gain or loss resulting from a change

in the fair value of a financial asset or financial liability must be recorded on the income statement. If it is a gain or loss on an available-for-sale financial asset, it must be recorded in "other comprehensive income." Dividends on an available-for-sale equity instrument must be recorded on the income statement when the company receives the right to receive payment.

IAS 39 requires that the company assess at the end of each accounting period whether there is any objective evidence that a financial asset is impaired.

IAS 39 divides "hedging" into three types:

- a "fair value hedge"
- a "cash flow hedge"
- a "hedge of a net investment in a foreign operation"

A "fair value hedge" is a hedge of the exposure to changes in fair value of an already recorded asset or liability that is attributable to a particular risk that could produce a gain or loss.

A "cash flow hedge" is a hedge of the exposure to variability in cash flows such as future interest payments on variable rate debt.

A "hedge of a net investment in a foreign operation" is defined in IAS 21 as the amount of the company's interest in the net assets of a foreign operation.

Summary of IAS 40: Investment Property

IAS 40 says that "investment property" is property, such as land or a building or both, acquired or leased with the intention of earning rental income or to be held in the hope it will increase in value. Investment property does not include property purchased for producing goods or supplying services, for administrative purposes, or to be sold as part of the company's usual business activity.

IAS 40 requires that an investment property must be recorded as an asset when, and only when, the investment property will probably produce future economic benefits which can be measured reliably. The cost of investment property must be recorded initially at its cost including transaction costs.

IAS 40 allows the company to choose to use either the "fair value model" or the "cost model" to record the value of investment property. The "fair value model" means that the company must record any changes in the fair value of the investment property in the income statement. The "cost model" (specified in IAS 16) requires an investment property to be measured after initial measurement at depreciated cost (less any accumulated impairment losses) along with disclosure of the fair value of the investment property. The fair value of the investment property is the price at which the property could be exchanged between knowledgeable, willing parties in an arm's length transaction.

IAS 40 requires that an investment property must be removed from the balance sheet when the investment property is disposed of or permanently withdrawn from use and no future economic benefits are expected. Gains or losses as a result of the disposal or retirement of investment property must be recorded in the income statement.

IAS 40 requires that the initial cost of a property held under a lease which classifies as a finance lease under IAS 17 must be recorded at the lower of the fair value of the property and the present value of the minimum lease payments. An equivalent amount must also be recorded as a liability.

Summary of IAS 41: Agriculture

IAS 41 applies to agricultural produce, which is the harvested product of a company's biological assets, only at the point of harvest. A "biological asset" is a living animal or plant, such as a cow or wheat. "Agricultural produce" is the "harvested" product of the company's biological assets.

IAS 41 does not deal with the processing of agricultural produce after harvest. It becomes inventory which is covered by IAS 2. For example, the processing of wheat into bread by a mill that has grown the wheat is governed by IAS 2.

According to IAS 41, "agricultural activity" is the management by a company of the processing of "biological assets", which includes growth, degeneration, production, and procreation, into "agricultural produce" available for sale.

IAS 41 requires that biological assets be recorded at "fair value" less estimated "point-of-sale costs." "Fair value" is the amount for which an asset could be exchanged, or a liability settled, between knowledgeable, willing parties in an arm's length transaction. "Point-of-sale costs" include commissions to brokers and dealers, levies by regulatory agencies and commodity exchanges, and transfer taxes and duties, but not transport and other costs necessary to get the biological assets to a market.

IAS 41 requires that a change in fair value less estimated point-of-sale costs of a biological asset must be reported in the income statement. In agricultural activity, a change in physical attributes of a living animal or plant may directly change the anticipated economic benefits (value) the company expects to receive.

IAS 41 does not apply to the land used for agriculture. Instead, IAS 16 Property, Plant and Equipment or IAS 40 Investment Property will apply, depending on how the land is classified.

IAS 41 requires that biological assets that are physically attached to land such as apple trees in an orchard are measured at their fair value less estimated point-of-sale costs separately from the land.

IAS 41 stipulates that an unconditional government grant related to a biological asset must be recorded as income when, and only when, the government grant is approved and becomes receivable.

IAS 41 requires that if a government grant is conditional, including where a government grant requires a company not to engage in specified agricultural activity, a company must record the government grant as income when, and only when, the conditions of the grant are met.

Summary of IFRS 1: First-time Adoption

IFRS 1 is designed to ensure that a company's first IFRS financial statement and any interim financial reports provide information that is easily understood by readers. It provides a starting point for the move from GAAP to IFRS at a reasonable cost and allows the readers to compare the two versions in the first year.

IFRS 1 requires that the company prepare an opening IFRS balance sheet (called the statement of financial position) as of the date of transition to IFRS. This opening balance sheet must comply with the standards in effect on the date of transition. It is not necessary that the company present this opening balance sheet in its first financial statements. Only the balance sheet dated at the end of the accounting period needs to be presented.

IFRS 1 sets out the steps in setting up the opening balance sheet:

1) Record all assets and liabilities as required by IFRS
2) Ensure that no assets or liabilities are recorded if prohibited by IFRS
3) Reclassify assets, liability, and equity items from GAAP to IFRS rules
4) Apply IFRS valuation rules to all assets and liabilities

IFRS allows exceptions to these rules if the cost of complying with IFRS outweighs the benefits provided to the readers of the financial statements (cost-benefit constraint under IFRS). This is especially true if prior period adjustments would require that management make judgments about past conditions and where the outcome is already known. For example, an outstanding court case would have to be reported as a contingent liability under GAAP in prior year statements but this year, the year of conversion to IFRS, the outcome has been decided. There would be no value in spending money to convert the contingent liability in the prior year statement to IFRS with regard to that particular item.

IFRS 1 requires disclosures that describe the effects of the transition from GAAP to IFRS on the company's balance sheet (statement of financial position), income statement (statement of results of operations), and cash flows (statement of cash flows).

Summary of IFRS 2: Share-based Payment

IFRS 2 requires that the company show the effects of share-based transactions in the income statement and on the balance sheet. Share-based transactions are transactions that involve payment, at least in part, in the form of company shares rather than cash. These include the granting of share options to employees and the transfer of shares and other equity instruments between related companies.

IFRS 2 says that companies who pay for goods or services received with shares must record an amount of shares equal to the fair market value of the goods or services received on the day they are received. If the fair market value of the goods or services received cannot be measured reliably, then the transaction is valued at the fair value of the shares.

If employees are providing services, and because it may be difficult to measure the market value of their services, IFRS 2 requires that the payment to employees be recorded at the value of the shares on the day of the transaction. If there is a vesting condition, such as 3 years of employment, the value assigned assumes that vesting will occur.

If the company incurs a liability that will be paid later in shares, then the value of the shares is used to record the liability. If payment extends beyond the accounting period, then the amount of the liability is adjusted in the next accounting period for any change in the value of the shares. Any gain or loss in the revaluation of the liability is recorded in the income statement.

If the company has a choice whether to make the

payment using cash or shares, it must record the amount of the liability as if it were going to be paid in cash.

IFRS 2 requires that the company must disclose the nature and extent of share-based payment arrangements that existed during the accounting period, how the company assigned a value to share-based transactions, and what was the effect of share-based payment transactions on the company's income statement and balance sheet.

Summary of IFRS 3: Business Combinations

A business combination is a merger or acquisition. Buying a partial group of assets and/or liabilities or the formation of a joint venture is not considered a business combination.

IFRS 3 requires that a company report the effect of any business combination in its financial statements in a way that enhances the clarity, relevance, reliability and comparability of the financial statements.

A company (the acquirer) that buys another company (the acquiree) that is not related must record the purchased assets and liabilities at their fair value on the effective date of the acquisition based on the terms of the purchase agreement and in line with the acquirer's accounting policies.

However, IFRS 3 requires some exceptions to this rule.

• Leases continue to be recorded based on their original contract terms.
• Any contingent liabilities that had been recorded by the acquiree will only be recorded by the acquirer if the obligation is probable and reliably measurable.
• Tax assets and liabilities must be recorded in accordance with IAS 12.
• Assets and liabilities related to employee benefits must be recorded using IAS 19.
• Any share-based payments must be recorded according to IFRS 2.
• Any non-current assets held for sale as well as assets and liabilities of discontinued operations must be

recorded according to IFRS 5.

• In a business combination, once all the assets and liabilities have been recorded, any difference is recorded as goodwill if the purchase price exceeds the recorded value of the assets and liabilities or as profit if the price paid is below the value of the purchased assets and liabilities.

IFRS 3 requires that the acquiring company disclose all information that will help readers of the financial statements evaluate the effects of the acquisition. Details of all adjustments to assets and liabilities and the policies used must also be disclosed.

Summary of IFRS 4: Insurance Contracts

IFRS 4 applies to companies that issue insurance contracts and defines an insurance contract as a contract where the insurer promises the policyholder to compensate the policyholder if a specified uncertain future event occurs, such as a fire or theft. IFRS 4 does not apply to the insurance company's financial assets and liabilities which fall under IAS 39.

Although IFRS in general would apply to all the contracts of the insurance company, including reinsurance contracts (reinsurance contracts involve providing coverage through the purchase of a policy from a second insurer), IFRS 4 permits the insurance company to introduce a policy of re-measuring every year particular insurance liabilities based on the prevailing market values at the time.

IFRS 4 prohibits insurance companies from setting up provisions for contracts that are being negotiated, but not yet signed. Insurance liabilities must be kept on the balance sheet until they are paid, cancelled, or expire, without offsetting them against any related reinsurance assets.

IFRS 4 requires that the company certify that it has recorded accurately its insurance liabilities and has performed an annual impairment test of its reinsurance assets.

IFRS 4 requires that insurance companies record insurance liabilities and estimated future management fee liabilities on a present-value-discounted basis. It also requires subsidiaries of insurance companies to apply the same policies as its mother company.

IFRS 4 requires that the insurance company disclose in its financial statements the amounts of its insurance contracts, as well as the amount, timing, and level of uncertainty of future cash flows from its insurance contracts.

Summary of IFRS 5: Non-current Assets Held for Sale and Discontinued Operations

IFRS 5 requires that a company classify as "held for sale" any non-current assets (sometimes called a disposal group) which management intends to sell or dispose of rather than use them up in business operations. The disposal group (discontinued operations) is a separate major line of business, a geographical area of operations, or a subsidiary that is acquired strictly for the purpose of reselling it.

The sale of the disposal group must be highly probable and offered at a price close to its current fair value and under terms that are normal for the circumstances. There must be an active sales plan in place to close the deal within a year.

IFRS 5 prevents disposal groups from being classified as held for sale if management intends to abandon the assets which will have no marketable value after they are used up. For example, it is sometimes cheaper to abandon old factories than to restore and sell them.

Summary of IFRS 6: Exploration for and Evaluation of Mineral Resources

IFRS 6 deals with financial reporting for the exploration and evaluation of mining resources. Spending on exploration and evaluation of mining resources is recorded as an expense until there is evidence that extraction is technicallly feasible and commercially viable.

Exploration activities are the search for mineral resources, such as oil, gas, gold, and diamonds, by companies who have a legal right to explore in a specific area.

IFRS 6 allows a company in the resource industry to continue, if it chooses, to use accounting policies in place just before switching to IFRS, but requires the company to perform an impairment test to see if the value of the exploration asset on the books needs to be adjusted down to the amount that will be recovered from that exploration asset. The impairment loss will be recorded in the income statement.

IFRS 6 requires that resource companies have an accounting policy to determine how it will set up cash generating units for impairment testing. This means the company can do a single impairment test for the whole group of assets in the cash generating unit instead of the more costly process of testing every asset in the group.

Triggers for impairment testing include:

• The expiry of exploration rights
• The lack of budgeting for exploration activities

- The decision to discontinue exploration activities
- Evidence that exploration costs will not be recovered in full even if it leads to successful development

IFRS 6 requires that the resource company disclose the amounts in the financial statements that are related to the exploration and evaluation of mining resources, how it arrived at those amounts, and the impact they have on the financial statements.

Summary of IFRS 7: Financial Instruments

IFRS 7 describes the disclosure requirements for companies with financial instruments on their balance sheet. Some companies such as manufacturers might only have a few included in accounts receivable and accounts payable, while other companies such as banks have most of their assets in the form of financial instruments such as financing agreements.

IFRS 7 requires that these companies present an evaluation of the relative importance of financial instruments on their balance sheet and income statement along with the risks associated with these financial instruments, both in quantitative and qualitative terms. In addition, management's plan to manage these risks must also be disclosed.

IFRS 7 does not dictate how the financial instruments are to be listed on the balance sheet. It leaves it up to the company to put them in logical groups based on their nature and provide enough information to understand how the company arrived at the amounts reported.

IAS 7 compliments the principles for recording, measuring and presenting financial assets and financial liabilities described in IAS 32 (Financial Instruments: Presentation) and in IAS 39 (Financial Instruments: Recognition and Measurement).

Summary of IFRS 8: Operating Segments

IFRS 8 specifies how a company should report financial and descriptive information about its "operating" segments in annual and interim financial statements. IFRS 8 defines an "operating" segment as a part of the business run by a CEO or equivalent that makes decisions about allocating resources and assessing performance. IFRS 8 requires that the internal reports used by the CEO to make these decisions be also prepared according to IFRS.

IFRS 8 specifies that the company present information by groups of similar products or services, about the countries in which it earns revenues and holds assets, and about major customers. It also requires that the company describe how it decided to separate this information.

IFRS 8 requires reconciliations of total segment revenues, total profit or loss, total assets, liabilities and equity amounts to corresponding amounts in the company's consolidated financial statements.

Finally, IFRS 8 requires that publicly-traded companies and their subsidiaries evaluate the nature and financial effects of their business activities and the economic environments in which they operate.

Staying up to date

9

Accounting standards are continually being revised and updated. To stay on top of any changes check out the following websites:

- Visit the International Accounting Standards Board (IASB) at **www.iasb.org** to sign up for automatic updates

- Visit the Securities and Exchange Commission (SEC) at **www.sec.gov** for the latest on IFRS

- Visit the American Institute of Certified Public Accountants (AICPA) at **www.aicpa.org** for the latest on IFRS

- Visit the Canadian Institute of Chartered Accountants (CICA) at **www.cica.ca** to sign up for automatic updates from the Canadian Accounting Standards Board

Index

About the Author

Mike Morley is a Certified Public Accountant (Illinois) who holds the top credit designations in the United States (CCE), Canada (FCI), and the U.K. (MICM). He is an internationally recognized authority in the field of finance with more than 25 years experience in credit, and collections.

A consultant, speaker, and author, his books and articles on business and finance have been published in the USA, Canada, the UK, and Australia.

Mike helps companies with cash flow problems get back on track. He also helps companies through the Sarbanes-Oxley implementation process by designing and testing internal controls in particular those related to credit and accounts receivable.

Mike can be reached by phone at **416-275-1278**, or by email at **mike@mikemorley.com**.

www.mikemorley.com

Other books by Mike Morley

"Financial Statement Analysis Simplified"

ISBN 978-0-9737470-5-8 translates the accounting language of financial statements into clear, easy-to-understand terms that anyone who needs to make well-informed financial decisions quickly will appreciate.

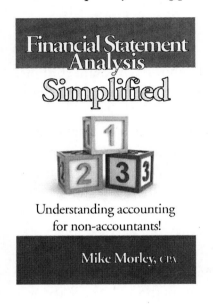

Understanding accounting
for non-accountants!

Mike Morley, CPA

1) Is it accurate?

2) Are you sure?

3) Can you prove it?

Mike Morley C.P.A.

"Sarbanes-Oxley Simplified"

ISBN 978-0-9737470-3-4 is an easy-to-read explanation of the requirements of the U.S. legislation that makes CEO's & CFO's personally responsible for the accuracy of their company's financial statements.

LaVergne, TN USA
01 March 2011
218289LV00004B/14/P